# A letter from the Series Editors

Dear Teacher,

This series of teachers' resource books has developed from Pilgrims' involvement in running courses for learners of English and for teachers and teacher trainers.

Our aim is to pass on ideas, techniques and practical activities which we know work in the classroom. Our authors, both Pilgrims teachers and like-minded colleagues in other organisations, present accounts of innovative procedures which will broaden the range of options available to teachers working within communicative and humanistic approaches.

We would be very interested to receive your impressions of the series. If you notice any omissions that we ought to rectify in future editions, or if you think of any interesting variations, please let us know. We will be glad to acknowledge all contributions that we are able to use.

*Seth Lindstromberg*
Series Editor

*Mario Rinvolucri*
Series Consultant

Pilgrims Language Courses
Canterbury
Kent
CT1 3HG
England

## Mario Rinvolucri

## Paul Davis

Mario Rinvolucri switched from journalism to EFL teaching at the age of twenty-five and since that time he has taught in Greece, Chile and the UK. For the last fourteen years Mario has worked for Pilgrims as a teacher, writer and teacher trainer. As a writer he seeks the warmth of collaboration. Among recent results of this habit are *Vocabulary*, with John Morgan (1986 OUP), *Dictation*, with Paul Davis (1988 CUP) and *The Q Book*, with John Morgan (1988 Longman). His current projects include a book to help teachers accept the inevitability and rightness of students translating from their mother tongue into the language they are learning and vice versa. Mario's most recent thrill has been finding new authors for the Pilgrims Longman Resource Books series.

Paul Davis comes from Birmingham and graduated from the Cambridge College of Arts and Technology. After one-to-one teaching of business English, supply teaching and ESL, he moved to the Cambridge Eurocentre, where he has been for the last ten years. He is an experienced teacher trainer and has taught ESP in the Basque country and in Venezuela. Paul has an RSA Certificate in Counselling in the Development of Learning and has a soft spot for Silent way teaching methodology. He is at present taking a year out, to live in Spain, to learn Spanish, and to write. Paul's previous publications include *Dictation*, with Mario Rinvolucri (1988 CUP) and various magazine articles. He is currently writing a History of the English language, with Felicity O'Dell.

## Dedication

To colleagues and students who have let us see feelings ranging from
firm self-trust to corrosive lack of confidence. You have opened our eyes.
Thanks.

Paul and Mario

# Contents

# Index of activities

# Introduction

*An introduction aims to bridge the gap between the authors of a book and the readers, and is normally written by the authors. We have asked a sympathetic reader and user of these materials, Barbara Garside, to introduce them to you. She sees the materials from the authors' point of view as well as from that of a reader – she is ideally placed to build a bridge between us and you.*

'Experience is what gives meaning to language.' (Gattegno 1972)

My first encounter with this book was about six months ago, when Paul gave me some of the language confidence activities to read. These were designed to develop students' feelings of self-assurance and ability to take responsibility for their own learning. I had a look, found them fascinating, and tried them out with one of my classes. The students, after a healthy dose of initial scepticism, enjoyed them enormously, benefiting greatly both from the language practice they provided and from their increased awareness of themselves as learners and as members of the group.

Some time later I read Paul's description of an experience of team teaching. Two teachers had presented the future forms to a group of students by having a staffroom style discussion in front of them, then inviting their questions. I was struck by the simplicity of this as a way of presenting language, as well as by the shift in teacher and learner roles it seemed to imply. The teachers were taking a risk by putting themselves on the line in front of the students, but doing this together enabled them to share their sense of vulnerability, ultimately increasing their inner strength and resources.

At this point I had no idea that the language confidence activities and the account of team teaching were in any way related. It wasn't until much later that I discovered that they were to be two parts of the same whole, and understood something of how they fitted together. They were both to feature in a book about confidence building for learners *and* teachers, as well as for teacher trainers and teacher development groups. According to Caleb Gattegno, educationalist and creator of the Silent Way, to whom in many ways this book is a homage, one of the biggest blocks to learning is lack of self-esteem. *The Confidence Book* seeks to build up self-esteem in both learners and teachers, by helping them to realise how much they already know, and to enjoy and draw on their own strength, feelings and experience.

I was fascinated by the idea that teachers might need to build up their confidence just as much as learners do, and that the two processes were inextricably linked. I thought it would be interesting to discuss it with a group of students, so I devised a questionnaire on 'confidence' for another teacher's Proficiency class. The students turned out to be very conscious of their own need for more confidence, especially in certain areas, such as listening, exams, vocabulary and fluency, but were quite amazed at the concept of confidence-building for teachers. They said that they derived strength from the teacher's apparent self-assurance and knowledge of the language. However, they seemed intrigued by my suggestion that they might derive a different, more lasting kind of strength from the teacher's admission of weakness, from seeing the teacher as a partner in the learning process rather than as someone to look up to or to try to emulate. I think this identification between learners and teachers, this sharing of real feelings – including negative ones such as anxiety, guilt and a sense of failure – is one of the keys to this book.

In the words of Gattegno, we need to 'consolidate the human dimensions of being, which include variety and individuality as essential factors for acceptance of others as contributors to one's own life', and in this case, learning.

## SIGN-POSTING
## A guide through the book

*The Confidence Book* is easy to use. Most of the activities require very little pre-lesson analysis or preparation – just an open mind (or a number of them) – and a desire to let things happen.

You could say that the book has its own natural order, progressing from students teaching each other their names, right through to teachers dealing with being observed. Within the part designed for learners (Chapters 1,3,4, and 5 and most of Chapter 2) there is also a sensible progression from the learning of discrete items such as words and sounds, to the more complex activities, or whole approaches, suggested by *Giving students control* (Chapter 5). The book could either be integrated into a standard syllabus or used separately in optional or extra lessons. It is perhaps worth pointing out that many of the activities are not 'one-off's', but can be used again and again, and built upon, as part of an ongoing process of learner and teacher development.

## Chapter 1 Language confidence

These are language confidence activities, which include work on sounds, vocabulary, grammar, reading, writing and conversation. This chapter is aimed at learners, via the teacher, whose role is to set up and facilitate the activity rather than impart information. In *Self-correction* (Activity 1.5), Paul and Mario quote Gattegno:

'Every student knows more than they think they know. Every student knows much more than the teacher thinks they know.'

This exercise, like many of the others in this section, emphasises the value of getting the text from the students, to lead them to a greater awareness of just how much they can achieve, even when they think they know very little.

In *Students present Grammar* (Activity 1.13), the class is divided into groups, who each prepare a grammatical presentation with the help of a grammar book. In subsequent lessons the groups teach each other their grammar area. There is no intervention from the teacher unless there is a need to clear up any doubts. This activity encourages students to think for themselves and to interact, and moves them away from dependence on the teacher.

## Chapter 2 Exams and tests

This chapter contains a number of activities devised to help with the anxiety often caused by exams, and two suggested solutions to the problems of pressure and artificiality which can be created by class-room observations.

For learners, many of the activities are aimed at getting inside the examiner's mind, leading to a greater understanding of the thinking behind exam questions. Sharing this understanding, and a sense of humour about it, can reduce learners' feelings of isolation and increase their ability to cope.

For teachers being observed, a shift in the roles of observer and observee is suggested, whereby both teach the same class and then discuss the results, or the teacher simply reports on a lesson rather than being watched. This makes the observation more of a genuine exchange of ideas and less of an inspection.

## Chapter 3 Listening to people

As the title suggests, this section is about listening to people. It moves teachers and learners right away from routine, non-interactive use of the tape-recorder towards an ability to listen for more than just surface message. Doing these activities and discussing them afterwards gives people a greater awareness of the richness and complexity of the listening process and redresses the over-emphasis so often placed on the speaking skill.

## Chapter 4 Energy from others

These physical activities can help put the group into the right frame of mind to undertake the activities in the other chapters of the book. They can build on the power and strength of the group without recourse to language.

## Chapter 5 Giving students control

This section is about handing over to students much of the responsibility for what goes on in class, both in fairly formal ways, as in *Negotiating discipline* (Activity 5.2) and *Student planning committees* (Activity 5.3), and in less formal ways, as in *Change of viewpoint* (Activity 5.7) and *What do they want from me?* (Activity 5.13).

In *Students' rights questionnaire* (Activity 5.1), group members decide how they feel about a series of individual rights and invent some rights of their own. In *The brilliance of one's own process* (Activity 5.4), students are asked to read a number of texts stuck on the wall outside, choose two or three and transcribe them inside the classroom, making as many journeys as they like. They then analyse and discuss the mental and physical processes they went through. Like many of the activities in this chapter, these help the students to become more aware of their learning processes and rhythms, and encourage them to share their feelings towards each other and the target language.

## Chapter 6 Interventions that have worked

Since I started writing this introduction, I have talked to several teachers about the book. Conversations usually run on the following lines: 'What's the book about?' 'Confidence.' 'Is it for teachers or students?' 'Both.' 'Oh good.' This indicates to me that teachers do perceive a need to build their own confidence, as well as to help their students to do so.

This chapter represents a major departure from the rest of the book, not only because it is aimed at teachers rather than learners, but also because it describes experiences rather than activities. There is a feeling of freshness and genuineness in these descriptions, which include ideas which have *not* worked as well as those which have. Users of the book get a real sense that they are sharing these teachers' experiences, and it can be very comforting to know that other people's ideas, like our own, are not always successful. From this we may derive reassurance and confidence ourselves.

## MY OWN EXPERIENCES OF THE BOOK

In the rationale for *Getting sounds right* (Activity 1.3), the authors say: 'There should be times when students are congratulated on what they get right'. This for me is a key point of the whole book, which I keep coming back to in my work as a teacher and teacher trainer. How much more effective it is to praise students and trainees for what they have done well than to criticise them for mistakes. I am constantly aware of this when giving feedback to teacher trainees or to students at the end of a fluency activity, where it seems particularly important not to dwell on the negative but to accentuate the positive.

I have used a number of activities from *The Confidence Book*, both with students and as a teacher trainer. I have found these sessions inspiring, rewarding and above all, a learning experience for me and the other participants. On an RSA Preparatory Certificate course, I tried out *Headchatter* (Activity 3.7) as an introduction to the listening skill. In this activity, participants talk for ninety seconds to their partners, who make a mark on a piece of paper every time they feel distracted. After discussing these distractions and possible reasons for them, they swap over. This turned out to be an extremely active and exciting lead-in to the listening process, which helped to establish a basis of trust between the trainees, while showing that it's all right not to be totally attentive all the time.

As tutor on an RSA Diploma course, I have used the *Speed writing* exercise (Activity 2.7) for exam practice, and an adaptation of *One-minute monologue* (Activity 3.1) for revision purposes. In *Speed writing*, teachers are given five minutes to write down everything they can think of about a topic; anything from auxiliary verbs to syllabuses. They then put their ideas together and into some kind of order, and within about fifteen to twenty minutes they each have the basis for a very comprehensive Diploma essay. At the same time, the process helps them to prepare for the rapid thinking and writing required in the exam. In my version of *One minute monologue*, participants talk to their partners for five minutes without interruption. They tell them everything they know about, for instance, stative and dynamic verbs or tense and aspect, and then swap. Some of the teachers on the course report that they have since started using this technique as a way of presenting or revising grammar with students. Thus an activity devised for learners has been adapted for use with teachers, and this adaptation further developed to create another, different, use with learners.

To me, this exemplifies the wonderfully rich, multi-layered and versatile nature of the book. It offers a wealth of very varied activities, many of which can be easily adapted to suit a wide range of aims and different types of group.

*Barbara Garside*
*Cambridge*
*September 1989*

## CHAPTER 1

# *Language confidence*

Many language learners either have or are induced into having a poor self-image. This can become a vicious circle: 'I am bad at learning this language, therefore I perform inadequately, therefore I am right to think I am hopeless at language.' The aim of this chapter is to offer you ways of allowing learners to appreciate their own achievements in areas such as pronunciation, vocabulary learning and coping with grammar.

Let's take an example: in *The power of the mother tongue* (p. 15) complete beginners listen to a story in their mother tongue with some target language words mixed into the text. They are then asked to write down any words they remember or *partly* remember. The stress is on inviting them to notice what they have got right, not what has gone wrong. People will get something like 90 per cent right and only focus on the 10 per cent that is wrong. This balance needs redressing, as guilt is an inefficient baseline from which to try and learn something.

In *100 verbs* (p. 14) students at a post beginner level are asked to estimate how many verbs they know. The lesson then shows them that they actually know two to four times more verbs than they thought they did. The aim throughout this section is to give people a positive, realistic assessment of their own abilities. If you, as the teacher, manage to get your students to realise how good they already are, this frequently leads to steep improvements in their performance. The message is not Moskowitz's 'accentuate the positive' (see *Caring and Sharing in the Foreign Language Classroom*, Moskowitz, 1978); it is much more simply 'allow yourself to notice the positive and to enjoy it'.

## 1.1

**LANGUAGE FOCUS**
Pronunciation

**LEVEL**
Beginner +

**TIME**
10–15 minutes

**MATERIALS**
None

**PREPARATION**
None

## THE FIRST VOCABULARY LESSON

### In class

This confidence-building idea is relevant in classes where people's names come from different cultures and/or languages, e.g. an adult education class learning English in Sweden that has a lot of refugees in it, or a mixed nationality EFL class in the USA.

1 Ask one student to face the group and pronounce their name loudly and clearly three times. Others round the group repeat and the student acts as teacher until most people can say the name properly. Then the student writes it on the board.

2 Continue round the group until each student has had a chance to teach the rest of the class to say their name. In each case the student writes the name on the board.

3 In the next class get people to revise the names. Insist that you and they pronounce each name to the satisfaction of its owner.

## RATIONALE

To say and spell another person's name correctly is not only a mark of respect to *them* but also an act of *self*-respect. To start a course with this exercise also introduces peer-teaching in an area where each of us is naturally a teacher: how our name should be said and written.

# SOUNDS AS GIFTS
## In class

1 Stand your class in a large circle. Miming very carefully, 'hand' your neighbour in the circle an imaginary object. They take it, aware of its size and weight. They can either hand the same object to their neighbour or change the object and hand that on. (At the end of this round you can ask each person to name the object they received and the object they gave – a hilarious vocabulary exercise.)

2 The object-handling serves as a lead-in to word-handling. Choose a sound the group has problems with, cup your hands and 'hand' the sound to your neighbour, saying it loudly and clearly at the same time. Cupping their hands, your neighbour takes the sound, turns to the next person in the circle, hands it to them and says the sound clearly. The handling and the saying are simultaneous. In this way the sound goes round the circle.

3 If a student gets the sound wrong, step out of your place in the circle and go over to the person who has just received the sound. Take it back from them and give it to the person *before* the one who got it wrong, saying it yourself loudly and clearly. They then give it to the mispronouncer who again hands it on, trying to say it correctly. If they are successful, return to your place in the circle. If they still say it wrong, repeat the procedure above.

## RATIONALE

Students offer each other sounds, words and phrases in the target language as gifts. At first students smile or giggle but it does not take long for the positive symbolism to become clear.

ACKNOWLEDGEMENT
We learnt the circle exercise from Joan Agosta (See Bibliography for details of published work).

### 1.2

**LANGUAGE FOCUS**
Pronunciation

**LEVEL**
Beginner +

**TIME**
10–20 minutes

**MATERIALS**
None

**PREPARATION**
None

## 1.3

**LANGUAGE FOCUS**
Pronunciation

**LEVEL**
Beginner +

**TIME**
20–30 minutes

**MATERIALS**
None

**PREPARATION**
None

# GETTING SOUNDS RIGHT

## In class

1 Model an easy English sound to the group. See who can repeat it almost perfectly. Model it again in a word. Again have some students repeat the word.
2 Tell the students there are many English sounds they produce almost perfectly. Ask them to work in pairs, to choose ten such sounds and write them down in the context of a word or phrase. They should choose sounds they think they get right, not sounds they find hard to produce.
3 Go round the class eliciting two words from each pair. Put the words up on the board, underlining the target sound. Tick all the sounds which the pair presenting them got reasonably right.

### RATIONALE

We spend too much time in class picking up dropped stitches. There should be times when students are congratulated on what they get right.

## 1.4

**LANGUAGE FOCUS**
Pronunciation

**LEVEL**
Beginner +

**TIME**
10–20 minutes

**MATERIALS**
A text at the right level for the students

**PREPARATION**
None

# THE HARDEST WORD

## In class

1 Ask the students, working on their own, to scan through the text and pick out the word or phrase they find hardest to pronounce.
2 Ask each student to dictate their word to you, which you write on the board, with your back to the class. If the student pronounces reasonably well, simply write the word up *without comment*.
3 If the student gets the word or phrase importantly wrong and those round the speaker do not usefully correct them, turn round, make eye contact and say: _____ (student's name), *make it more English!* The student tries again. If it is still wrong, repeat your exhortation, giving the student the feeling they *can* get it right without technical help.
4 If the student is still unable to get the pronunciation right, give them the opposite command: *Make it more Italian/German/Portuguese!* (depending on the student's mother tongue). Sometimes, paradoxically, this command helps the student to get the sound right. If this does not happen and the student has literally obeyed your instruction, simply say *Now do the opposite!*

### RATIONALE

Your initial position is with your back to the group. You are refusing to mother them – you are throwing them onto their own resources. When they get things right you do not praise or comment.

By asking the students to 'make it more English', you are telling them they have the resources to get it right. If you have to repeat this instruction, the group may see you as bullying/persecuting one of them and will offer plenty of support, including useful peer-correction.

By asking the students to 'make it more foreign' you are paradoxically changing frame, and this sometimes unlocks the right answer. The process outlined above is one version of what Caleb Gattegno called 'forcing awareness'.

# SELF-CORRECTION

## In class

1 Ask the students to go through the text and each choose a favourite sentence. Have one of the students read their sentence aloud. Listen carefully to the whole sentence and if it has not been said near perfectly, ask the student to repeat it. Continue to ask for repetition until it is near perfect. Do not model the correct forms yourself. If the student in question, and the rest of the group, are unable to hear a particular problem then write the sentence on the board and indicate whereabouts the difficulty lies. Do not model the correct form.
2 Repeat this process with half-a-dozen members of the class.
3 For this correction technique to work well, a number of things are necessary:
   - You should be neutral and unaggressive.
   - You should treat all the students equally (don't accept a shoddy performance from a student you perceive to be poor).
   - You need to persevere – if you give up on a student before they get it right they can get extremely discouraged.
   - There needs to be some trust in the group – the students need to realise that by not spoonfeeding, you are helping, not just being perverse.

### RATIONALE

The only real and lasting form of correction is self-correction. If you model the correct form, students can imitate the modelling and feel cosy doing this. This does not mean that they can now monitor the difference between their mistake and the correct form, nor that they will get it right next time. The above procedure can, initially, feel frustrating to some students. In the longer term it makes self-evident sense.

### ACKNOWLEDGEMENT

'Every student knows more than they think they know.'
'Every student knows much more than the teacher thinks they know.'
These axioms and the self-correction technique come from *Teaching foreign languages in schools* (Gattegno 1972).

**1.5**

**LANGUAGE FOCUS**
Pronunciation

**LEVEL**
Beginner +

**TIME**
10–15 minutes

**MATERIALS**
A short text – it can be from the coursebook

**PREPARATION**
None

## 1.6

**LANGUAGE FOCUS**
Pronunciation

**LEVEL**
Beginner – lower intermediate

**TIME**
15–30 minutes

**MATERIALS**
None

**PREPARATION**
Previous exposure to everyday situational dialogues, probably from the coursebook

# MOUTHING

## In class

1 Remind the students of dialogues they have worked on. Ask someone to come out and mime such a dialogue with you. No language should be used.
2 Replay the scene. This time you speak and the student mouths their part.
3 Have everybody work on the dialogue in pairs. Both sides mouth. The room should be full of language and virtually silent.
4 Ask the students if there are any bits of language they couldn't find, and give help.

### RATIONALE

For some people, the jump from listening to a language to actually articulating things in it is a breathtaking one. This exercise builds confidence by allowing people to speak but without making tell-tale sounds.

### VARIATIONS

Have one pair mime a scene of their own creation. No words should be spoken. All the others then role play the same scene but with words spoken out loud. They practise their role plays and then each pair performs the role play for the class group.

ACKNOWLEDGEMENT
We learnt the variation from André Fonck, who works for l'Office de l'Emploi in Belgium.

## 1.7

**LANGUAGE FOCUS**
Pronunciation

**LEVEL**
Beginner – elementary

**TIME**
15–30 minutes

**MATERIALS**
A pointer or a stick

**PREPARATION**
None

# INDEPENDENT DATES

## In class

1 Copy the chart on the next page onto the blackboard. It represents all you need to elicit the dates in English from your students.
2 Suppose you want to get the students to produce 'the tenth of December'. Simply tap the square at the bottom of the left hand column and then the circle at the bottom of the right hand column. A sensible date to start with is today's. Use the pointer to tap out stress and rhythm. Don't speak – allow the students to find the words. Without speech, guide them to produce the right words and sounds. There will be a lot of peer-teaching, with students hypothesising and helping each other. You may occasionally have to give a spoken model. Do this clearly and once only. Students soon get used to listening for the few things you *do* say when you say little or nothing.

| DATES | MONTHS |
|-------|--------|
| ○ ○ ○ ◇ | ○ |
| ○ ○ ○ | ○ |
| ○ ○ ○ | ○ |
| ○ ○ ○ | ○ |
| □ □ □ | ○ |
| ○ ○ ○ | ○ |
| ○ ○ ○ | ○ |
| ○ ○ ○ | ○ |
| ○ ○ ○ | ○ |
| □ □ □ | ○ |
|  | ○ |
|  | ○ |

*Fig. 1*

**3** You make the exercise more human if you work on significant dates like feasts, birthdays, etc.

**4** After some practice with you in control, get students to come out and use the chart and pointer to give each other 'date dictations'.

## RATIONALE

With your voice no longer spoonfeeding them, low level students soon start listening more actively and taking responsibility. When you drastically reduce the amount of vocal modelling you offer them, you also reduce their dependence on you. From a feeling of responsibility and independence comes a sense of well-being and confidence.

ACKNOWLEDGEMENT
This exercise derives from the Silent Way approach of Caleb Gattegno. You will find more exercises of this sort in *Dictation* (Davis and Rinvolucri 1988).

## 1.8

**LANGUAGE FOCUS**
Vocabulary

**LEVEL**
Beginner +

**TIME**
15–30 minutes to explain
10–15 minutes in later classes

**MATERIALS**
A set of cards and a card index box for each student

**PREPARATION**
None

# FORGETTING WORDS AND REMEMBERING THEM

## In class

1 First, set up the system. Ask the students to work individually and write down three words each in each of these categories:
Words I firmly know
Words I have forgotten
Less recent words I know
Recent words I know
(To find these, ask them to go back over the earlier units of their coursebook or over recent reading materials.)

2 Ask the students to compare the words in their four categories.

3 They now copy their four sets of three words onto cards, one word per card. These cards are then arranged in four sections in the card index boxes as shown in Fig 2. Invite them to experiment with the way they put the words on the cards. There are a number of ways shown in Fig. 3 on the opposite page.

4 A regular homework task would be to get the students to put new words learnt in a previous lesson or lessons on cards and file them in their boxes.

REVISION
Ask the students to work through a given section to check if the words should currently be in that section. If a student finds a word in *Words firmly known* that they don't know, then it goes into *Words forgotten*. If they know a word on looking through *Words forgotten* then maybe it should go in *Words firmly known*. Words need to migrate from *Recent*

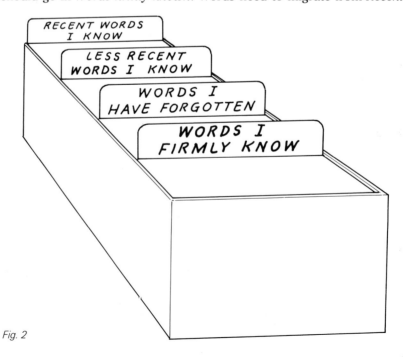

*Fig. 2*

*words* to *Less recent words*. Sometimes a student can confidently move a word from *Recent words* to *Words firmly known*. This work can be done individually or in small groups.

a) Picture

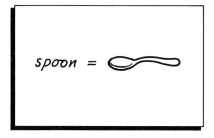

b) Double contextualisation

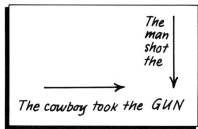

Mother tongue translation of GUN on the back of the card

c) Affective response

I don't like TUESDAY. I confuse it with Thursday.

The text on this card would be in mother tongue. Translation of Tuesday on the back of the card

d) Designing the word

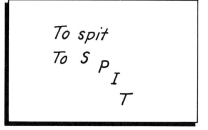

The student has graphically designed the word to resemble the action

*Fig. 3*

## RATIONALE

Remembering, forgetting and re-remembering are normal learning events and this kind of storage system accepts this. It takes the guilt out of forgetting. Students have the right to forget what you 'taught' them since, if they forget, you never really taught them it. You sent out but they did not significantly take in. The sub-text here is 'forgetting is fine – we all do it'. The *Words forgotten* category is a complex one and students come to different understandings of what should go in there.

## ACKNOWLEDGEMENT

Dierk Andresen taught us this procedure. You will find plenty more word retention techniques in *Vocabulary* (Morgan and Rinvolucri 1986).

## 1.9

**LANGUAGE FOCUS**
Vocabulary

**LEVEL**
Beginner

**TIME**
Lesson 1: 5 minutes
Lesson 2: 30–50 minutes
Lesson 3: 30–40 minutes
Lesson 4: 50 minutes

**MATERIALS**
None

**PREPARATION**
None

# 100 VERBS

## In class

LESSON 1
At the end of a lesson ask each person in the group: *How many verbs do you know in English?* Don't comment on the answers, and ask them to think about the question for homework.

LESSON 2
1 At the start of the next lesson ask them the same question again. (In some of our classes they have revised their estimates downwards.)
2 Mime a simple verb. Have the students say it and designate one of them as class secretary, who will write down all the verbs found by the class on a single sheet of paper. Ask each student in turn to mime a verb which the group then tries to say. If no one knows the verb in English, refrain from teaching it. The worse the mimes the more verbs they generate. Keep the activity going until you reach a good round figure like 50, 100 or 150. Take in the secretary's verb list.

LESSON 3
1 Give everybody a copy of the verb list and ask the students to work individually to categorise the verbs in any way they wish. They must establish at least two categories, and fewer categories than the number of words on the list. The students are to give their categories headings.
2 Ask them to explain their categorisations to each other in pairs or small groups.

LESSON 4
(This may come a lot later in the course.)
1 When the students start work on past tense forms, ask them to refer to the group verb list. Divide them into four teams. Each team, working with reference books, pulls out verbs belonging to their designated category:
Team A: verbs that form the past with /d/ e.g. *listened*
Team B: verbs that form the past with /t/ e.g. *worked*
Team C: verbs that form the past with /ɪd/ e.g. *landed*
Team D: irregular verbs e.g. *went*
2 When the teams have finished ask them to regroup in fours with one person from each team in each foursome. They compare categories.

**RATIONALE**

Some students wildly underestimate what they know in the language they are learning. The idea in this exercise is to have it dawn on them how *much* they already know, both individually and collectively. In one class where they finally came up with 135 verbs, they initially thought they knew between ten and twenty. Of course we beg lots of questions by referring to 'knowing words'; the exercise above is simplistic but a real morale booster all the same.

ACKNOWLEDGEMENT
The categorisation exercise suggested for the third lesson above comes from the work of Caleb Gattegno. For further ideas in this area of vocabulary teaching see *Vocabulary* (Morgan and Rinvolucri 1986, Sections D and G).

# THE POWER OF THE MOTHER TONGUE

## Before class

Choose a story you know well to tell bilingually. In this example we are assuming English as the learners' mother tongue and Greek as the target language.

*Once upon a time there was an 'ikoyenia,' a father, a mother and a three-year-old 'pethi'. They all lived together in a little 'spiti' that stood on the main street of the village.*

In your case the story will be mostly in the students' mother tongue with a few words of English introduced in such a way that they are understandable from context, or glossed with a translation.

### IN CLASS

1  Tell the bilingual story right through.
2  If you are teaching teenagers or adults, ask the students to write down any words or parts of words that they remember. A 'part of a word' might be a single sound, a syllable, an intonation pattern without a clear memory of the sounds involved, etc. Stress to the group that you are very interested in the bits of words they remember as well as in the whole words or phrases.
3  Using the students' mother tongue, ask them to read out what they have written. Encourage them to share partly remembered words as well as full ones. (If you are teaching young children, move straight to the oral recall of the words – omit the writing stage.)

### RATIONALE

Beginners frequently underestimate the complexity of what they are doing when they first approach a new language. As a result, they fail to give themselves credit for real achievements like remembering and reproducing an intonation pattern just because they can't remember the individual sounds. They end up blaming themselves for not retaining the sounds rather than feeling good about what they have achieved.

The same goes for words they remember eighty percent right. Most learners will focus on the twenty percent that is wrong and give themselves little credit for the eighty percent. This exercise aims to create a better, more balanced, more realistic self-awareness in beginners. You learn more if you value your achievements than if you focus on failings.

**1.10**

**LANGUAGE FOCUS**
Vocabulary; for use with monolingual classes

**LEVEL**
Beginner

**TIME**
20–30 minutes

**MATERIALS**
None

**PREPARATION**
Think of a suitable story to tell bilingually

## 1.11

**LANGUAGE FOCUS**
Vocabulary

**LEVEL**
Post-beginner +

**TIME**
20–30 minutes

**MATERIALS**
Reading materials

**PREPARATION**
Choose the phrases

# CONFIDENCE WITH PHRASES
## Before class

Choose words and phrases from reading material your class is currently dealing with. Be ready to tell your own anecdotes and experiences around the phrases with a view to stimulating similar reactions from the students.

### IN CLASS

1 Ask the students to underline in the reading material the words/ phrases you want to work on.
2 Tell them an anecdote of your own about the first one. Elicit similar stories from them.
3 Continue in the same way with the other words/phrases. For example, Mario had a text with these two phrases in it: *polluted air, fumes from cars*.

First he told his group a story about a chip-pan fire in his house: the kitchen was full of *heavily polluted air*. Others then spoke of '*polluted air*' in their experience.

Then he told the group how he likes *fumes from cars* when cycling in London in winter. The fumes provide a form of outdoor central heating. Others in the group told their '*fumes from cars*' experiences.

### RATIONALE

It is common to hear a colleague complain that they taught the students all the words they needed for a role play and then they simply did not use any of them in the event. They fell back on simpler ways of expressing themselves, used old words or got by without using verbal language at all.

It would seem that a student needs to get over the shock of meeting a new word or phrase. The person needs to domesticate it, tame it, make it their own before venturing to use it. The exercise proposed here is a personalising of new words and an initial group owning of them. Somehow it seems that something has to happen between first meeting new vocabulary and using it.

# TRUST YOUR MEMORY
## In class

1 Divide the students into circles of ten to fifteen people.
2 Ask each person to bring to mind something they are good at doing or happy doing.

   The first student in each group gives their name and mentions an activity they are good at: *I'm Heidi, I'm good at gardening*. The second student in that group repeats the Heidi information and also mentions something they are confident about: *Heidi's happy gardening. I'm Tonia and I'm good at shooting* . . . The third student runs through what the first two have said and adds what they are good at. The activity continues until the last student in the circle repeats all the information about everybody else before saying what they themselves are good at. Do not allow writing!
3 Ask the groups how many ideas the last person in each circle had to remember.

### NOTE

One of our students panicked at the thought of saying she was confident about anything. Her sister was a famous model in her country and good at everything. One of her friends in the group finally helped her decide that she was good at two things: keeping secrets, and dressing young to get half-price tickets!

**1.12**

**LANGUAGE FOCUS**
Grammar; adjective + gerund

**LEVEL**
Post-beginner +

**TIME**
10–15 minutes

**MATERIALS**
None

**PREPARATION**
None

# STUDENTS PRESENT GRAMMAR
## In class

1 Give out copies of the chosen grammar book and group the students in teams of five. Ask each team to concentrate on one grammar area and to produce a coherent presentation of it. Tell them they will later have to present this area to the whole class. Leave the room so they don't have you hovering and 'helping'.
2 In subsequent lessons the teams teach the areas of grammar they have been assigned. Do not intervene during the student-led lessons. Only trouble shoot at the end.
3 Follow up with the whole group doing an exercise or two from the grammar book.

### RATIONALE

This is a powerfully useful exercise as it encourages student independence and allows the students to interact in a frame you have set, but *without* you. You find out a lot about their real understanding of grammar and the students become more realistic in their expectations.

**1.13**

**LANGUAGE FOCUS**
Grammar

**LEVEL**
Elementary +

**TIME**
One 45 minute period
Several 15–30 minute slots in subsequent lessons

**MATERIALS**
Copies of a learner's grammar

**PREPARATION**
Pick one area of grammar per five students

*A Basic English Grammar* (Eastwood and Mackin OUP 1982) is suitable at elementary level but the exercise is clearly cross-level and other books would be suitable at other levels, for example: intermediate: *Practical English Usage* (Michael Swan OUP 1980); advanced: *Talking of Grammar* (Roger Bowers Longman 1987).

## 1.14

**LANGUAGE FOCUS**
Grammar

**LEVEL**
Beginner – lower intermediate

**TIME**
30–40 minutes

**MATERIALS**
None

**PREPARATION**
None

# THE ONES I GET RIGHT

## In class

1 Ask the students to work in pairs. They are to write:
   **a** five four-word sentences in English
   **b** four six-word sentences in English
   **c** three nine-word sentences in English
   Tell them to go for what they know and are sure of.
2 Ask the pairs to compare their sentences with each other. There may be disagreements as to whether a sentence is correct. Get them to write any doubtful sentences up on the board. Do *not* give your verdict at this stage, though they may demand it.
3 Get the whole class to have a look at the dubious sentences picked by the students themselves. In the end they may come to voting on the correctness or not of a sentence. Only when this has happened give your verdict. Do not deal with wrong sentences none of the students have spotted as being wrong. Work on these problems in a later lesson.

### RATIONALE

This exercise allows low level students to compare the criteria they have in their heads with the way the target language is. It allows them to examine their basic grammatical notions and see which of these are still inter-language and which properly belong to the target language. For you it is a gift of a diagnostic exercise.

### NOTE

Stand back and enjoy watching the students discuss, write, think and argue. Keep out of the process. If you join in you will guillotine the whole thing. They will often try and draw you in to swing authority behind their particular contention. Stay out.

# CORRECTING NATIVE SPEAKERS
## In class

1 Ask the students what kind of mistakes small children make in their mother tongue(s). Things like regularising past tenses, reversing sound sequences (e.g. in French, *masagin* for *magasin*) and inventing new words are likely to come up.
2 Explain that small English-speaking children do exactly the same. Give out the 'Two-year-olds' story sheet' and ask them to correct the childrens' grammar.

### RATIONALE

Advanced students of English sometimes mention the 'tyranny of the native speaker'. They are continually called upon to notice and imitate the linguistic antics of this frequently idealised being.

Young native speakers use an inter-language not dissimilar to foreign learners of the language. Chinese and Turkish learners feel quite in tune with article omission! When you are an adolescent or adult learner of English there is an element of playful revenge in correcting a two-year-old's grammar, especially when it resembles your own!

### Two-year-olds' story sheet

**Cass G.** (*2 years, 8 months*)
Boy fell out of car. He went in car again. He fell in water.

**Daniel W.** (*2 years, 10 months*).
Little boy played. He cried. He's all right. He went home. He went to bed. When he wakes up you're gonna say goodnight to him.

**Daniel W.** (*2 years, 11 months*).
He broke it. He's OK. He didn't broke it. It's all right. The little boy fixed it.

**Donna R.** (*2 years, 8 months*).
Girl swimmed. Got all wet. She cried. Her feets got in water. Her mommy got there. She picked her up. She stopped crying. She fell in the water again. She fell in the water again. Her mommy picked her up again. She said, 'Don't cry'.

**Bernard H.** (*3 years, 6 months*).
Once there was a lion. He eat people. A fish come. The fish swimmed. The lion ate the fish. The lion ate another fish. Then he went to sleep. He woke up.

© Longman Group UK Ltd 1990

(These narratives are taken from *Children tell stories* Pitcher and Prelinger 1969).

## 1.15

**LANGUAGE FOCUS**
Grammar

**LEVEL**
Post-beginner – lower intermediate

**TIME**
15–20 minutes

**MATERIALS**
One copy of the 'Two year-olds' story sheet' for each student

**PREPARATION**
None

## 1.16

**LANGUAGE FOCUS**
Reading

**LEVEL**
Post-beginner +

**TIME**
Preparation: 20–40 minutes
In class: 45 minutes

**MATERIALS**
None

**PREPARATION**
Interview one of your students

# STORY ENRICHMENT
## Before class

Ask one of the students to tell you a story about themselves, making clear that it will be used as reading material by the whole class. Interview the student outside class time. Write up the story, respecting the student's way of telling it but in such a way that it is a real reading task for the others. Alternatively get one student to write out a story about themself and rewrite it to the right level of reading difficulty for the group.

### IN CLASS

Use the student's story text with whatever range of reading comprehension techniques you find useful.

With some classes we have made sure the storyteller understood her story in the rewritten form, asked her to give it out to the class and herself run the lesson. With some groups it is best to slip out of the room and leave them to it.

### RATIONALE

For some students it is a great boost to see a story of their own in correct English and shared with the class. The build-up of student stories over a period of weeks documents the time spent together, and revising the stories shows how well remembered these stories are compared to textbook reading passages. (One way we revised them was to pick a sentence from one and a phrase from another and ask students to identify the stories.)

Here is an example of two stories told by post-beginner students. The first one we sang to the tune of 'My Bonnie Lies Over the Ocean'!

## Oh bring back my money to me!

I telexed the . . . School to find out
If the fees would be dollars or pounds
They told me the fees were in dollars
In dollars, in dollars not pounds.

Chorus:  Oh bring back, bring back,
         Bring back my money to me, to me . . .

But the fees they were really in pounds
So I went to the bank and I lost
Two per cent of commission they took
Two per cent of commission they took.

Chorus

I telexed my brother for money
For money I had not enough
I telexed my brother for money
And he sent me a mountain of pounds.

Chorus

## My father's stroke

My father was a farmer – he owned 200 hectares of land.
In 1980 he was fifty-two.
He usually smoked forty cigarettes a day.
We lived in a town in European Turkey.
It was Wednesday, December 15th.
We were having dinner with the TV on.
It must have been about 6.00 p.m.
Suddenly my father looked strange. One eye shut and one eye stayed open.
He slumped in his chair.
He had a stroke.
I rushed for a doctor.
It took me fifteen minutes by taxi, there and back.
The doctor said he was dead.
He was dead – it was Wednesday night in December, eight years ago.

ACKNOWLEDGEMENT
This is a time-honoured primary school technique. We got the idea of applying it in the EFL classroom from Lou Spaventa (See Bibliography for details of published work).

# REAL TEXTS FOR BEGINNERS

## In class

**1.17**

**LANGUAGE FOCUS**
Reading

1  Check on reading problems the students have with the texts on the next page.
2  Split the students into threes and ask each group to choose two of the readings to illustrate with frozen scenes (group sculptures). Give them ten minutes to prepare and to rehearse.
3  Four or five groups then present their scenes to the whole class.

**LEVEL**
Beginner – elementary

### RATIONALE

**TIME**
15–30 minutes

Most of the texts offered to low-level students are 'realistic' but 'unreal'. A dialogue about buying a railway ticket is realistic in the sense that this is something the student may one day want to do via English. In the classroom it is unreal, because the student is not at that moment going on a journey. A lot of beginners' work is incessant rehearsal for some hazy future reality. The text choice in this unit is literary and will affect some students in a direct, here and now, 'gut' way. There is every reason to use powerful, person-relevant text with beginners. It makes the language come home to them – it makes them feel they can own the words and ways of saying things.

**MATERIALS**
One copy of the 'Szkutnik readings' for each student

**PREPARATION**
Ask the students to prepare the readings for homework, looking up new words, etc.

## The Szkutnik readings

### Separation
I am here. You are there. Here and there. You and I. A long way apart.

### A rich person
I am a rich person. I have plans. I have hopes. I have dreams. It's a pity that I have no money, no time and no energy.

### You have no time
So we won't meet today. You can't. You have no time. Something very important. I know, something more important than me.

### Goodbye
Goodbye. Be happy. Forget me. Don't write. Don't think. Don't come back. Be happy. Goodnight.

### I don't want to change
I am simple. You are different. You want me to change. But I don't want to change. I want to be as I am. I don't want to be a scientist. I don't want to be a manager. I don't want a career. . . I only want to have time for thinking.

### I've lost my glasses
My watch has stopped. My compass is broken. I've lost my glasses. I'm in a desert. Alone. I think it's called the Sahara.

### You know what I mean
She has such eyes. I can't describe them. She blushes in such a way, you know what I mean. And she smiles in such a way. And she walks in such a way. I feel . . . I can't find the words.

© Longman Group UK Ltd 1990

ACKNOWLEDGEMENT
The texts are all taken from *Thinking in English* (Szkutnik 1986).

# THE OAK AND THE IVY
## In class

1 Ask each student to tear the four sheets of paper into eight half pages.
2 Tell the group you and they are going to work silently for a few minutes writing letters to each other about whatever they like. Each letter is to be addressed to someone in the group, and should be signed. When a student finishes a letter they deliver it. A person receiving a letter is free to answer it or not. Join in the writing exercise yourself.
3 The exercise is hard to bring to a close. People get involved.

### RATIONALE

In order not to interfere with the trusting, easy, natural modelling process it is vital that the teacher should have the confidence not to venture corrections of the student's letter. If you *do* correct such letters you are encouraging accuracy at the cost of adventurous, innovative use of language. You are also tampering with the natural flow of the correspondence between you and the student. For this exercise it is better to be a nurturing parent than a censorious one.

In your correspondence you are the oak and the student is the ivy. The linguistically weaker writer naturally twines round the stronger one's text, borrowing, testing and trying things out. This is a totally natural and uncontrived communication situation.

I wrote to a student, Antonio, about how he was feeling after four weeks in the UK (I was not the regular class teacher) and also how he was feeling about being away from his business in Spain. This was his reply:

## 1.18

**LANGUAGE FOCUS**
Writing

**LEVEL**
Post-beginner +

**TIME**
20–40 minutes

**MATERIALS**
Four A4 sheets of paper for each student

**PREPARATION**
None

> Dear Mario,
>
> I'm now here in England and I find it's very quiet and sometimes I remember my country but not my business because I know that I must ~~gone~~ back to Spain and I find another time my business.
>
> Your Antonio

*Fig. 4*

I wrote back to him and used these three abstract nouns in my letter: *quietness, relief, bustle.* In his answer, writing both naturally and unconsciously, Antonio used the words I had offered him:

> Dear Mario –
>
> <u>Quietness</u> can be also the atmospher and not only the person In my case I'm very <u>relief</u> here in England but I mean that when I'm going to Spain I know that I must work with full of <u>Bustle</u> and Doesn't matter.
>
> Your Antonio

*Fig. 5*

He uses *quietness* correctly, while the other two refuse to fit neatly into the grammar frame he puts round them. It doesn't matter. He uses the words confidently to say what he wants to say and his inter-language has been given a nudge forward. Adequate grammatical digestion of the words will come later.

## VARIATIONS

Rather than write letters in class you can write individual letters to students, with them and you doing it as homework. This has a powerful modelling effect and it can be very humanly satisfying. We have found that each letter takes about fifteen minutes to deal with, so it is important to calculate how much time you personally want to give to the exercise, but it is usually quicker and more enjoyable than marking homework.

ACKNOWLEDGEMENTS
We learnt the in-class letter writing from two colleagues at ESIEE in Paris, Mike Gradwell and Krys Markowski. They picked it up from therapy practice. The variation is an idea from *Writing, Maths and Games in the Open Classroom* (Kohl 1977). The idea is also outlined in *Writing* (Hedge 1988).

# FROM BEHIND A MASK

## PREPARATION

As homework, ask each student to write between forty and fifty things about themselves between the ages of five and fifteen. Tell them this material will be private.

## IN CLASS

1 Suggest to the group that novelists often draw on experiences from their own lives to create characters. Ask each student to create a new character based on the elements they drew from their own life and to imagine the situation the character is in. The students are to write about their characters in any way they wish.
2 The writings are shared round the group.

## RATIONALE

Some students are blocked if asked to write directly about themselves, despite this being the bedrock of their experience. In this technique they are asked to write about a character external to themselves but who is created from within their own personal experience. The character they create acts as a mask. Masks bring some people a great deal of confidence – just think of carnival time!

ACKNOWLEDGEMENT
We learnt this idea from Travis Venters at the JALT convention in Kobe, Autumn 1988.

## 1.19

**LANGUAGE FOCUS**
Writing

**LEVEL**
Lower intermediate +

**TIME**
Preparation: 60 minutes
In class: 60–90 minutes

**MATERIALS**
None

# ROLE PLAYING HARD SITUATIONS

## In class

1 Ask each student to give examples of things they find hard to do in English. Here are some of the things our students came up with:
- answering the phone
- making international phone calls
- giving their opinions in front of other people
- explaining again when the first explanation was unclear
- maintaining a long conversation with a native speaker
2 Explain to your students that one way of coping with linguistically hard situations is to rehearse them in role play. Ask for a volunteer to role play one of their own feared situations.
There are two ways of running the role play:
a Have the protagonist student choose someone in the group to play the other person in the conversation. At the beginning of this process the two of them will have to reverse roles several times so that the helper student finds out how to play the role assigned.

## 1.20

**LANGUAGE FOCUS**
Conversation

**LEVEL**
Elementary +

**TIME**
30–65 minutes

**MATERIALS**
None

**PREPARATION**
None

**b** Have the student sit opposite an empty chair. When they are on their own chair they are themselves. When on the other chair, they are the other person. The student shifts back and forth.

In both these role play formats, encourage students in the group to make their language suggestions, but to make them 'in role' by going behind one of the speakers and speaking as that speaker. In this way the protagonist student feels the help and support of others in the group. Here is an example of how this situation can work.

One of our students wanted to go and visit her boyfriend for the weekend. She knew her parents would be phoning and wanted her landlady to say she was not available without saying where she had gone. She felt embarrassed at asking her landlady to lie to her parents.

## VARIATIONS

Role plays can be used to rehearse a difficult situation. They can also be used to help a student gain new understanding of a hard situation they have been through.

We watched such a role play in an ESL context in West London. A Bengali boy had been accused of losing a valuable bag of plumbing tools by his instructor at technical college. The instructor was very angry and the boy felt he had been wrongly accused. In the ESL class the boy role played the instructor and was partly able to see things from his point of view. The role play and the support of his classmates helped the student to come to terms with this negative experience.

## NOTE

This exercise is particularly relevant to students on courses in an English-speaking country.

# CHAPTER 2

# *Exams and tests*

What stops you feeling confident? Being judged, being isolated and feeling you have no control over what's happening to you. This is exactly what happens to students taking an exam. As teachers we do our best to equip our students with the language to pass exams and we all have tips ready and spend time with students trying to alleviate the worries that students have when faced with exams. And we've all been through them ourselves. In this section we offer techniques to help you to continue to help your students.

In *Good exams* (p. 27) students are asked through a simple question-naire and writing exercise to tell each other their exam experiences and break down the isolation they may sometimes feel. *Students set an exam* (p. 32) asks the students to have a go at writing their own exam questions. By doing so they can get a clearer view of the process they have to go through and so feel more in control. Finally, offering the students a chance at self-assessment in *The confident placement test* (p. 36) gives the students an alternative to being judged by others.

## GOOD EXAMS

### In class

1 Give out the questionnaire and ask each student to complete the sentence stems either as themselves or as someone they know well who likes exams – a brother, sister, a friend.
2 Get the students to form threes and compare their completed sentences.
3 Each student then chooses someone else's sentence that they like and puts it up on the board.

ACKNOWLEDGEMENT
Annie Oakes used sentence stems like these at Eurocentre in preparing students for the Cambridge exams.

## 2.1

**LEVEL**
Lower intermediate +

**TIME**
15–25 minutes

**MATERIALS**
One copy of the Good exams questionnaire for each student

**PREPARATION**
None

### Good exams questionnaire

Exams are _____

My best exam was _____

My funniest exam was _____

I can remember an exam when _____

My most surprising exam was _____

It would be good if exams were _____

I would do better in exams if _____

Exams in English should be _____

© Longman Group UK Ltd 1990

## 2.2

**LEVEL**
Lower intermediate –
advanced

**TIME**
40 minutes

**MATERIALS**
None

# EXAM ANXIETY

### PREPARATION

Find a nervous person who, despite their anxiety, is *willing* to speak to your class on a topic of their choice.

## In class

1 The speaker talks to the class for ten to fifteen minutes. The speaker is thanked and goes.
2 Ask the group what they noticed about them. Elicit from the class what gave away the anxiety, the stress, the nervousness. Look at the gesture, stance, eye movements, voice.
3 Ask the class to work in small groups and bring back to mind test and exam situations in which they have felt nervous. Also ask them to explain how they did or did not cope with the situation.

### NOTE

One of the scary things about exams is the feeling that you have to face the problem alone. This exercise allows students to share with others and realise that others also go through parallel emotions. Sometimes students offer each other excellent tips: in one class a twenty-year-old French girl described the final oral in her travel agency exams. There were two examiners, both of them professionals from the trade. She imagined both of them sitting naked on the lavatory. This vision melted her tension away and she got properly into her stride!

# A BAD EXAM
## In class

**2.3**

**LEVEL**
Lower
intermediate +;
teacher trainees

**TIME**
30–40 minutes

**MATERIALS**
One copy of
Longfellow's 'The
rainy day' for each
student

**PREPARATION**
None

1 Give out 'The rainy day' and ask the students to learn it by heart for the next class. Tell them to get it word perfect – there will be a test on it.
2 In the next class have all the students sit either facing the walls or facing the back of the room. Bring out four victims to sit at the front of the class, facing the front. One by one they recite the poem to the blackboard.
3 You mark them out of 100. Take off thirty marks for not finishing the recitation within a thirty-five second time limit. (It is hard to fit a decent reading into thirty-five seconds.) Take off marks according to the following marking scheme:

Words omitted or wrong:                 5 marks
Words mispronounced or wrongly stressed:   4 marks
Hesitations:                         3 marks
Omissions of *s* at the end of words:     10 marks
*Pass mark: 50*

4 Ask the class to resume normal seating. Announce the victims' scores and write up your marking scheme. A discussion should ensue on the absurdity of this test and its marking scheme.

### The rainy day

The day is cold, and dark, and dreary;
It rains, and the wind is never weary;
The vine still clings to the mouldering wall,
But at every gust the dead leaves fall,
   And the day is dark and dreary.
My life is cold, and dark, and dreary;
It rains, and the wind is never weary;
My thoughts still cling to the mouldering past,
But the hopes of youth fall thick in the blast,
   And the days are dark and dreary.

Be still, sad heart! and cease repining;
Behind the clouds is the sun still shining;
Thy fate is the common fate of all,
Into each life some rain must fall,
   Some days must be dark and dreary.

© Longman Group UK Ltd 1990

(from *The Poetical Works of Henry H. Longfellow* 1982 Suttaby and Co.)

## RATIONALE

In preparing students for exams and tests it is essential that they realise how odd and arbitrary these are. Students often do realise, in quiet, unexpressed ways, but it does good to bring these feelings out into the open. Among the hundreds of thousands of German Abitur students penalised for omission of third person *s* there must have been some who wondered why this particular slip should be considered a mortal sin by their teachers. When professionals act in seemingly arbitrary and irrational ways it is important that their clients/victims should reach a mature understanding of this.

## 2.4

**LEVEL**
Intermediate +

**TIME**
20–30 minutes

**MATERIALS**
A copy of the June 88 FCE exams of the decontextualised multiple choice sentences of the sort you get in the Cambridge First Certificate in English

**PREPARATION**
None

# DEALING WITH MULTIPLE CHOICE

## In class

1 Give out the sheet of ten sentences from the June 88 First Certificate in English Reading Comprehension paper. Ask the students, in pairs, to choose the items the examiners expect them to choose but to also pick out all the other possible ones and to provide contexts in which they would be possible. Give the group these examples:

a I'd rather you _____ your dog outside.
   A leave   B left   C leaving   D to leave

C and D are grammatically impossible. B is the one the examiner wants because in the grammar of EFL. *I'd rather* . . . is followed by a stem + *ed* form (past). A is not what the examiner wants but is quite possible; the register is direct and fairly familiar.

b How _____ of you to bring presents for everyone!
   A grateful   B hopeful   C successful   D thoughtful

The examiner is expecting the answer to be D for two reasons: i) *thoughtful* slots into the phrase with the neatness of a cliché; ii) a student who thinks *thoughtful* means pensive will not choose it.
   But *How hopeful of you to bring presents for everyone* could well be said by a sarcastic speaker who feels the presents are being offered to curry favour. And C might be said by a sarcastic speaker to a person who normally forgets to offer people presents.

2 When the students have picked the items the examiner wants and the other possible-in-context items, bring the group together and compare notes.

## RATIONALE

This way of dealing with decontextualised multiple choice sentences in class allows the students to evaluate the examination paper. It puts them in a position of power over the paper. It trains students to realise that, though the examiner only wants one choice, the language is a much more open system than the exam.

You will find that the firm reasons for ruling out a particular multiple choice item are either grammatical or collocational. If the choice is mainly semantic there are often contexts in which two, three or even all the items will fit.

This critical way of viewing past papers in class enables students to have a much better go at pleasing the examiner in the exam itself.

## FCE June 1988

1 I'll come over to lunch when I _____ typing this report.
   A have finished   B will have finished   C had finished
   D having finished

2 I'd rather you _____ your dog outside.
   A leave   B left   C leaving   D to leave

3 Did you remember _____ the letters.
   A post   B having posted   C to post   D to have posted

4 I can pronounce that word but I can't _____ it.
   A mean   B spell   C describe   D say

5 Susan looked _____ to see who had come into the office.
   A for   B after   C up   D out of

6 How _____ of you to bring presents for everyone!
   A grateful   B hopeful   C successful   D thoughtful

7 It was very kind of you to bring me flowers, but you _____ have done it.
   A don't need   B needn't   C hadn't to   D oughtn't

8 I returned home to _____ some papers I had forgotten.
   A take   B bring   C gather   D fetch

9 It was hot yesterday but today's _____ hotter.
   A more   B less   C even   D also

10 They're _____ arriving at six o'clock, but we don't know whether they're coming by coach or train.
   A absolutely   B surely   C presently   D certainly

© University of Cambridge Local Examinations Syndicate 1988

# 2.5

**LEVEL**
Post-beginner + (the example given is upper intermediate)

**TIME**
First class: 20–30 minutes
Second class: 15–20 minutes

**MATERIALS**
A reading passage with test items but without multiple choice components – the one offered here is taken from Cambridge FCE, June 1988

**PREPARATION**
Students need experience of past papers with reading comprehension multiple choice questions

# STUDENTS SET AN EXAM

## In class

LESSON 1

**1** Explain to the students that you are giving them a reading passage with comprehension items but without the multiple choice components. Ask them to work in threes and to invent their own sets of four multiple choice components; one is the correct answer and the other three are distractors. Do one with the class to make sure everybody has the task clear.

**2** The students produce five sets of multiple choice items.

LESSON 2

**1** The students do each others' tests. Compare results.

**2** Let the students compare their items to those originally set by the Cambridge examiners.

### RATIONALE

By creating a part of an exam paper the students put themselves in the examiners' shoes. They are simultaneously getting one over on the examiners and empathising with them. Students enjoy the exercise in the same way that play-goers like going behind the scenes and seeing things a bit from the actors' point of view.

### VARIATIONS

If you normally write an end-of-month test for your students, why not hand it over to them? Divide the class into, say, five teams and ask each team to create one fifth of the test. You take in their work and correct it.

The students then all sit the four fifths of the test that they did not create. Each team marks their fifth of the exam.

Writing their own test is a major way of getting people to revise the work they have recently done. In the frame proposed you have to check the tests created by the sub-groups, but you save yourself the drudgery of writing a test and of then correcting the students' papers.

ACKNOWLEDGEMENT
We learnt the variation above from Jean-Paul Creton (See Bibliography for details of published work.)

## FCE reading passage

### Notes on Your New Driving Licence

1 We (like other countries in the European Community) are now issuing new-look driving licences. Your licence is in the new-style but there has been no change to the driving licence groups or duration of licences. Old-style green licences will stay valid up to the date shown on them. They will not be replaced before that date unless a new licence needs to be issued (e.g. following a change of address).

2 Please check the licence carefully. If you think everything is correct, sign it in ink and put it in the wallet provided so that the name and address can be seen. If you think anything is wrong, please send the licence back to the Department, stating what you think is wrong. Your licence runs from the date you asked for it to begin or the date your valid application reached the Department, if later.

3 Whenever you telephone or write to the Department about your licence always give your Driver Number, which is on the front of the licence. The Driver Number helps us to find your record. It contains the first five letters of your surname, your date of birth in coded form and the initial letters of your forenames plus other characters which are unique to you. Make a note of your licence details below in case you lose the licence. Then keep this leaflet in a safe place.

### Fees

The fee you have already paid will cover the cost of all future renewals. But you will need to pay a fee for:

■ a duplicate licence;
■ removing endorsements;
■ adding permission to ride a motorcycle (as a learner).

1 What is the leaflet for?
  A
  B
  C
  D

2 Drivers who have old-style licences
  A
  B
  C
  D

3 The licence should be
  A
  B
  C
  D

4 You must pay extra if you
  A
  B
  C
  D

5 The leaflet is for people who have
  A
  B
  C
  D

© University of Cambridge Local Examinations Syndicate 1988

## Questions set by FCE examiners

1 What is the leaflet for?
  A to tell you how to apply for a new licence.
  B to give more information about the new licences.
  C to be used as a driving licence if the original is lost.
  D to explain the new traffic laws in the European Community.

2 Drivers who have old-style licences
  A must exchange them immediately for new-style licences.
  B must apply for a new-style licence before the date shown.
  C will receive a new-style licence if they move house.
  D should write to the Department for a new Driver Number.

3 The licence should be
  A returned to the Department after it has been signed.
  B returned to the Department if any information is incorrect.
  C renewed every year.
  D kept with the signature visible.

4 You must pay extra if you
  A renew your licence.
  B buy a new car.
  C take up motorcycling.
  D have a road accident.

5 The leaflet is for people who have
  A special licences.
  B old-style licences.
  C new-style licences.
  D lost their licence.

© University of Cambridge Local Examinations Syndicate 1988

## 2.6 INVISIBLE PICTURES

**In class**

LEVEL
Post-beginner +

TIME
10–15 minutes

MATERIALS
None

PREPARATION
None

1 Ask students to bring to mind a picture that they know very well – it could be a snapshot, a poster, a book illustration – the main thing is their familiarity with it.
2 Group them in threes, A, B and C. A has a timed two minutes to describe their picture to B and C. B and C are asked to listen and only intervene if they really don't understand the speaker. The listeners then get another timed two minutes between them to describe to A the way they imagine A's picture.
3 Using the same procedure, B and C describe their pictures.

**RATIONALE**

This is specifically useful in preparing for the oral section of the Cambridge FCE exam. In this exam, candidates are asked to talk about a picture the examiner gives them. In the exercise above you have them describe a powerfully familiar picture – the need to talk is provided by the fact that the listeners do not have the picture in front of them. The absence of the physical image facilitates visualisation on the part of both speaker and listeners.

ACKNOWLEDGEMENT

We learnt this exercise from John Morgan (See Bibliography for details of published work).

# SPEED WRITING

## In class

1 Lead the group in an energy raising, one-minute physical exercise (see Chapter 4 p. 47).
2 Tell them to sit down and to write for four minutes on a topic you give them. This is a competition to see who can write the most words in four minutes. The words must be in meaningful sentences. Time them. Then ask them to add up their words and shout out the numbers.
3 Lead the group in a second short physical exercise that relieves the tension of fast writing. Ask them to write again, this time for a timed three and a half minutes. Tell them to write about anything they like. They add up the words and shout out the number.
4 Give them a final three-minute speed writing stint. This time pre-scribe a topic.
5 Ask everybody to revise their three bits of writing and read them to their neighbours.
6 The first time you do this exercise, allow time for feedback. The exercise appeals to some students a lot while others will dislike it.

**RATIONALE**

For some students a bout of speed writing at the start of a written composition exam is an excellent way of letting ideas come up from below spontaneously. The technique stops students thinking about what might go wrong and loosens constraints. The concentration involved frees students from the nerves of those around them in the exam room. This is the case for some students, not all.

ACKNOWLEDGEMENT

We learnt this technique from Katie Plumb.

**2.7**

LEVEL
Lower intermediate +

TIME
30–40 minutes

MATERIALS
None

PREPARATION
None

## 2.8

**LEVEL**
Beginner +

**MATERIALS**
None

**PREPARATION**
None

# SHARING THE MARKS

## In class

Explain to the students that you want them to revise for the next class test in groups of three. Organise them, if possible, so that there is a good, an average and a poor student in each threesome. Explain to the students that although they will do the test individually, each person in a given threesome will receive the average of their own mark and the marks of the other two, e.g. if A gets 60%, B 40% and C 27% each of them will receive 42.33%.

### RATIONALE

This testing system makes helping the weaker students part of the stronger students' self-interest. It reduces the loneliness and isolation of the test situation. It puts the stronger students in an elder sibling position and shoves them into a teaching role. They can often be better at this than the teacher.

We have met teachers who cannot accept the way this form of testing subordinates the individual to the group. The very idea of it makes them see red. Wide acceptance of this system would go a long way towards making secondary schools less lonely and competitive places.

ACKNOWLEDGEMENT
We heard about this technique from Vincent Broderick who works in Osaka. The system has been tried in one or two places in Japan. The idea was also mentioned in *Practical English Teaching* (Spring 1988).

## 2.9

**LEVEL**
Beginner +

**TIME**
90 minutes

**MATERIALS**
None

# THE CONFIDENT PLACEMENT TEST

### PREPARATION

Six large signs to stick on the walls to divide the students into class groups, as follows: Very advanced; Advanced; Upper intermediate; Intermediate; Lower intermediate; Beginners.

## In class

1 Assemble the students (not more than 100) in the largest open space you have available in the school. After welcomings and announcements, tell the students that they have ninety minutes before being split up into class groups. For the first thirty-five minutes they will do warm-up exercises.
2 Each person from the teaching team then leads a short warm-up exercise. These should involve movement and plenty of short bouts of talking with many different people. A classic example of such an exercise is *Inner circle – Outer circle*. Half the group forms a circle

facing outwards (everyone on their feet); the other half of the group forms an outer circle facing inwards.

Each person should have a partner in the other circle. For one minute the partners introduce themselves to each other. The inner circle is then asked to move round two people to the right, while the outer circle stays still. Each person now has a new partner in the other circle. A minute is allowed for mime introductions; no speaking permitted. At the end of the minute people are given another minute to check out the information they have derived from the mimes by talking to their partner. Four or five rounds of the game are played with different communication tasks given for each round.

3 After thirty-five to forty minutes of warm-ups, ask the class teachers to put up their signs in order round the walls of the room with 'Very advanced' at one end of the scale and 'Beginners' at the other. Each class teacher stands below the appropriate sign.

4 Explain to the group that they are now going to choose their level and their class. Explain how important it is that they take time over this and get it as near right as they can. Also tell them that this morning's decisions are not irrevocable and that class changes will be allowed. Their task is to go to the level that they think suits them and then to talk to everybody else who has come to this group and also to the class teacher. Tell them to take a good half hour over this. Explain that if they reckon they have chosen the wrong group they should go either up or down and again start talking to each person in this new group. The responsibility is theirs. The class teacher's role in this process will be to try and get a linguistically reasonably homogenous group, but she will also have the age and sex mix in mind. You and the other teachers should be ready to cope calmly with a certain amount of disorientation and chaos at this point. To many students the whole idea of placing themselves is novel and to some quite worrying.

5 Once the class teacher sees that a reasonably homogenous group of the right size seems to be forming, they may want to do a short oral exercise with them to further check their impression of the students' oral abilities (see Chapter 3, *Listening to people*).

6 The students go off to class with their class teachers.

ADVANTAGES
- The students take responsibility for their course from the word go.
- The warm-ups and the placement process are highly social; this is in stark contrast to the freezing, deadening effects of written tests.
- The time taken to place students is short.
- There is no deadening marking to be done by the teachers.
- This method of placement is about as inaccurate as more formal testing. Since some people come on courses not having used English for several years while others are in it up to their ears there is no hope of any first-day placement procedure being accurate. So accuracy of class placement should not be too great a worry, and the

inevitability of class changes over the first two days of the course has to be accepted.

■ Students are free to choose their groups using a whole range of inner criteria of which language ability will only be one.

DISADVANTAGES

■ In a range of six to eight levels the upper and lower groups seem to form easily but there is a lot of student and teacher uncertainty in the middle of the ability range.

■ Some teachers and students are worried at the openness and informality of the procedure.

■ You can't work this system with more than one hundred plus students – it gets too unwieldy. If you have two hundred people to cope with, they have to be processed in two batches.

Barbara, a German teacher of English, came on a language refresher course at Pilgrims. The thirty teachers involved did a couple of warm-up exercises and were then asked to divide themselves into two groups: 'Very advanced' and 'Advanced'. The language tutors left the room for twenty minutes while this was going on. Barbara placed herself in the lower group, through both tutors privately agreed that her language level 'should' have put her in the upper group. They did nothing to influence her decision, though they worried about it.

At the end of the two week course Barbara wrote this about her aims and her process:

Aim:     To regain my self-confidence and my speaking skills.

Process: At the beginning I felt very uncertain as to the level of my language skills. I did not want to be too much exposed because I had not been able to come up to my own expectations for the past five years. Considering my age and my duties I felt I should be better. But after the first three days I felt more confident and did no longer question everything I said . . .'

It was a good thing that we offered no 'objective' test to force Barbara into the wrong group for her image of herself. She stayed in the 'lower' group and accepted the disadvantages and advantages of her decision.

ACKNOWLEDGEMENT
This form of testing, which is frequently used on Pilgrims Summer Courses, was first introduced to us by Lou Spaventa (See Bibliography for details of published work).

## 2.10 BEING INSPECTED

While the rest of this chapter aims to help your students when their work is being scrutinised, this page is about how you can engineer more useful ways of having superiors inspect and evaluate your classes, be they government inspectors, directors of studies or senior colleagues.

### THE INSPECTOR SUBSTITUTE-TEACHES

Ask the inspector to teach your class, while you take a free period. Brief the inspector carefully beforehand.

After the lesson spend half an hour with the inspector so that they can find out all the things they now want to know about the class and individual students.

During this interview the inspector is comparing their genuine experience of teaching with your own. How better can they get an untrammelled picture of you teaching this particular group? They have not sat in the back of the classroom, pretending to be unthreatening and in fact upsetting all the normal patterns of the group.

### THE INSPECTOR LISTENS TO AN UNSEEN LESSON

Ask the inspector to meet you after one of your classes. Spend half an hour uninterruptedly reporting exactly how the lesson went, how you feel about the students, how this lesson fits into the sequence of lessons you have given, etc. The inspector's task is to listen as empathetically as they can, trying to see things powerfully from your point of view. Since they did not see the lesson they are relatively unburdened by their own preferences and prejudices. With luck you will feel yourself talking to a senior friend rather than to an avenging angel.

### NOTE

For further thoughts on an inspector mirroring the teacher's account of a lesson see Rinvolucri's article 'A Role Switching Exercise in Teacher Training' in *Modern English Teacher* (Spring 1988).

# CHAPTER 3

# *Listening to people*

You're in a crowded room, with lots of conversations going on at once. Over a deafening hubbub of voices you're managing to listen to the interesting words of the person you're chatting to. Suddenly your attention switches to the far side of the room. Someone has whispered your name. Maybe they're gossiping about you or paying you a compliment. You want to hear. And you can.

It's clear that listening is about more than understanding the words that are used. In this chapter we try to deal with the other aspects of successful listening – paying your best attention, empathy with the speaker, observation, feeling you are being respected, having space for people to listen to you. When we say to ourselves 'nobody ever listens to me' we don't mean that they don't understand the words we use. The exercises in this section are about listening not to language but to content, not to tapes but to people.

## 3.1

**LEVEL**
Post-beginner +

**TIME**
15–20 minutes

**MATERIALS**
None

**PREPARATION**
None

## ONE-MINUTE MONOLOGUE

### In class

1 Pair the students and explain that each of them will have sixty seconds to speak to the other. The topic is open. Explain that after the paired monologues they will report one thing the other said to the whole group. During each monologue the listener is to respond *without* speaking.
2 Ask them to decide who will speak first. Time the first minute. When it's over ask the second speaker to start, again for sixty seconds.
3 Each student reports one thing said by their partner to the whole group.

### RATIONALE

Offering a time limit to a person speaking a foreign language will often reduce their anxiety. *It can't be that bad if I only have to speak for a minute.*

The exercise as outlined above is good a) as an ice-breaker and b) as a way for you to gauge the group's mood. For both these purposes it is good to leave the topic open.

### VARIATIONS

1 You can also use the exercise to focus students in on a topic or on a significant area of it. Suppose the theme proposed by the coursebook you are using is 'pollution', you could usefully organise one-minute

monologues on 'ways people in my family pollute the environment'.

2 We have also used the exercise as a preparation for oral exams.

3 After you've done this exercise two or three times for one minute and the students have got used to the format, gradually increase the time limit to two minutes, then three, then four. This is an excellent way of providing fluency work for beginner/elementary classes or classes of a higher level who find extended speech a problem.

ACKNOWLEDGEMENT

We first came across this type of exercise through a co-counselling course run by Fenella Butler.

# REPORTED SPEECH CONVERSATION

## In class

Pair the students and invite them to have a conversation on a topic of their mutual choice. A starts talking. Before B can intervene and make the point they may want to make, they have to paraphrase/repeat what A has just said. B should start off with a reporting verb and continue *without* backshift: *You said you feel a bit anxious about these exams because* . . . B then carries on the conversation until A wants to intervene. This intervention is preceded by a repetition of what B has just said, and so on.

### RATIONALE

Exercises in reflective listening like the one above allow students to notice the other person from the other's point of view, a full and stimulating experience.

### VARIATIONS

You can introduce this kind of reformulation procedure into a traditional debate. The first speaker moves the motion: *This house believes that Thatcherism makes the poor poorer.* When the person opposing the motion stands up to speak, their first task is to summarise the first speaker's ideas to their satisfaction. They then proceed with their own speech. The third speaker, seconding the motion, has to summarise the opposition arguments to the opposer's satisfaction, etc.

It has been seriously suggested that this procedure would remove fifty per cent of the areas of disagreement at superpower negotiations. The suggestion is that fifty per cent of their disagreements are mis-reading of the other side's words.

## 3.2

**LEVEL**
Post-beginner +

**TIME**
10–15 minutes

**MATERIALS**
None

**PREPARATION**
None

## 3.3

**LEVEL**
Lower
intermediate +

**TIME**
15–30 minutes

**MATERIALS**
None

**PREPARATION**
None

# PUTTING PEOPLE DOWN
## In class

**1** Put these 'model conversations' up on the board:

**A:** Nobody cares whether I am dead or alive.
**B:** I do, I wish you were dead.

**A:** I don't know enough words.
**B:** Oh, you mean vocabulary.

**2** Pair the students and ask them to produce a couple of 'put-down' dialogues like the ones above in which B is hostile to and totally out of tune with A. Ask them to practise saying them convincingly.
**3** Get the pairs to play the dialogues to the whole group.

### RATIONALE

This exercise focuses on empathetic listening by having students explore its opposite. You may want to use it in conjunction with more conventional activities from this section.

### ACKNOWLEDGEMENT
We learnt this exercise and the one that follows at a workshop on 'Six Category Intervention Analysis' run by James Kilty and Sharon Kilty, from the University of Surrey.

## 3.4

**LEVEL**
Post-beginner +

**TIME**
20–30 minutes

**MATERIALS**
None

**PREPARATION**
None

# I AM A PERSON WHO . . .
## In class

**1** The students work in pairs and one of them speaks for four minutes while the other listens without interruption. Each of the speaker's sentences opens with: *I am a person who . . .* You time the four minutes.
**2** The listening students then have four minutes to reproduce (not necessarily in the same order) all the sentences produced by the speaker. The reproduction should be in the first person so that they are acting as a mirror to the speaker. You can expect the listener to remember nearly all the sentences.
**3** Repeat the exercise with the roles reversed.

### RATIONALE

This is a very simple exercise that boosts students' confidence in their own powers of recall. People are amazed at how much they are able to remember.

The insistent refrain *I am a person who . . .* strongly affirms person-hood.

If the speaker is poorer at the target language than the listener, some effective language correction takes place when the listener feeds back the sentences, effective because it is usually unintentional and therefore unthreatening.

## QUESTIONS WORTH ANSWERING
### In class

1 Ask the students to work in threes with A facing B and C. For a timed minute A asks B and C as many questions as they can on a topic given by the teacher. B and C's task is to listen and remember as many of the questions as possible. They do not take notes. The topic could be you as a student, you as a worker, you as a family member.
2 B and C then have three timed minutes to answer any of A's questions they want to. A's task is to listen to the answers attentively and without interruption.
3 Repeat the exercise with B and then C taking on the questioner role.

#### RATIONALE

This exercise combines attentive listening with medium term remembering. If, as A, you have asked a stream of questions and B and C have rememberd and decided to answer several of them, you feel confirmed. By answering, they are validating your thinking. It enhances self-esteem to feel that another person has listened to you carefully and bothered to remember what you said.

**3.5**

**LEVEL**
Post-beginner +

**TIME**
10–15 minutes

**MATERIALS**
None

**PREPARATION**
None

## CONTROLLING THE QUESTIONS
### In class

1 Working on their own, students jot down twelve roles they have or had in life, e.g. sister, lacrosse captain, comforter, colleague, aunt. This list is private to each person.
2 From the twelve roles, ask them to choose six they are willing to share information about. They write two questions addressed to themselves about each of the six roles. The questions should be ones they can give interesting answers to.
3 Ask them to work in pairs, swapping questionnaires, so that A puts B's questions to B and vice versa.

**3.6**

**LEVEL**
Lower intermediate +

**TIME**
20–30 minutes

**MATERIALS**
None

**PREPARATION**
None

**RATIONALE**

This is one of a number of exercises around the interrogative forms in which the person answering the question controls the content of the question. It is a self-disclosure exercise in which the subjects have plenty of time to decide how much to show of themselves. Having control tends to breed confidence.

ACKNOWLEDGEMENT

We first encountered this type of activity in *Caring and Sharing in the Foreign Language Classroom* (Moskowitz 1978).

## 3.7

**LEVEL**
Lower intermediate +

**TIME**
10–15 minutes

**MATERIALS**
None

**PREPARATION**
None

# HEADCHATTER

## In class

1 Pair the students and ask A to speak for ninety seconds on a topic chosen by B. It must be a topic A feels happy with.
2 While A talks, B has a pencil at the ready. They make a mark on the paper every time they think of anything that leads them away from what A is saying. This could be a train of thought started by A's speech, it could be a background noise and an association with it, it could be a totally unconnected own thought.
3 When A finishes the minute and a half, B tells A all the distractions and sideways thoughts they have had.
4 Repeat the exercise the other way round.

**RATIONALE**

To share with another the degree to which you find it hard to follow their train of thought establishes a basis of trust.

ACKNOWLEDGEMENT

We learnt the exercise above from Mike Lavery (See Bibliography for details of published work).

## 3.8

**LEVEL**
Intermediate +

**TIME**
10–15 minutes

**MATERIALS**
None

**PREPARATION**
None

# DESCRIBING THE OTHER

## In class

1 Pair the students. Tell them they are going to spend seven minutes observing things about each other, imagining things about each other *and* checking out if their observation and imagining is felt to be accurate by the other person.
2 A starts off and after a few seconds looking carefully at B, might say: *I observe you looking upwards and tapping your foot. I imagine this means you are feeling a bit bored and embarrassed.* After each of A's statements, B either affirms by nodding or disagrees by shaking their

head. B does not need to use words for this.

3 They then work the other way round, with B observing A. They do as many rounds of observing and imagining as they can in the seven minutes.

4 Allow time for people to discuss the exercise in their pairs or in larger sub-groups.

## RATIONALE

This kind of work enhances group cohesion and allows people to break through an embarrassment threshold. The first time you do this exercise there is likely to be a certain amount of self-consciousness and silliness. For some it may be the first conscious introduction to the world of the non-spoken.

ACKNOWLEDGEMENT
We learnt this exercise at a workshop on 'Six Category Intervention Analysis' run by James Kilty and Sharon Kilty from the University of Surrey.

# THE POWER OF LISTENING

## In class

While all the other activities in this chapter are aimed mainly at helping students to become better listeners, this one is for sensitising teachers to arguably the most important part of our trade: empathetic listening. The aim of this training session scenario is to introduce the concept of listening to the person and not simply to the message at its surface level.

1 Ask people to work in groups of three. Tell them to spend thirty to sixty seconds bringing to mind everyday life situations in which they take pleasure in listening, in which listening is not a strain or an effort. Give them an example of your own. Explain that each person will speak for ninety seconds on pleasurable listening situations – the task of the listeners is to pay as much attention as they can, to stay *with* the speaker and not to get sidetracked. The listeners may want to prompt the speaker but it is vital they help them to follow their train of thought, not the listeners' own. Each person will have a ninety-second turn at speaking.

2 Ask each group of three to choose the first speaker. Each person in the group speaks for ninety seconds, which you should time accurately. Start and finish everyone at the same time. Then ask everybody to spend three to five minutes writing a diary entry on how well or badly they listened, on what stopped them listening, on the bits that were easy to listen to, etc. Tell them the diary will be private.

**3.9**

**LEVEL**
Teacher training

**TIME**
50–60 minutes

**MATERIALS**
None

**PREPARATION**
None

3 The trainees now make new groups of three. They spend thirty to sixty seconds silently bringing to mind how they organise their own listening in class. Again model, telling them some of what you do to organise your listening in class. Now ask them to speak and listen again, following the same system as above. Then ask everybody to spend three to five minutes writing another private diary entry about how they felt as speaker in both the above sessions. Did they talk equally to both listeners, how much did they feel attended to, what physical indications made this plain to them?

4 Now form new groups of three. Ask them to think of instances in their everyday life in which intense empathetic listening has a strong positive effect on those round the listener. Offer the group an example from your own life. The trainees again speak and listen in three sessions of ninety seconds. They write a diary entry on what they feel about this odd form of timed counselling listening they have been engaged in.

5 Each person now picks a partner of their choice and goes off for a feedback walk and finally, the session ends with a general plenary discussion.

## RATIONALE

By listening fully to students, teachers can give them added confidence – the message is clear: *I am really paying attention because what you are saying is inevitably significant at one level or another.*

## VARIATIONS

We have used the same frame with language students. We asked them to speak about the following themes in four 'rounds': childhood, teenage, middle age, old age. The diary suggestion was that they should briefly note down the ideas in the two other people's speaking that had most interested them after the first session – the last diary entry was about the feelings the exercise left them with. The frame is a useful one with uneasy late teenage classes. Everybody speaks – some people listen for some of the time.

ACKNOWLEDGEMENT
Both the content and the process of the teacher training exercise is *with attention* listening. You are *doing* and *reflecting on* precisely the same thing. We found this concept hard to grasp when we first met it. Here's another example: PEN TA SYL LA BIC has five syllables and means five syllabled. The form of the word and its meaning content are identical. We learnt the idea of applying two-levelledness from *Models and Metaphors in English Language Teaching* (Woodward 1990).

# CHAPTER 4

# *Energy from others*

Discipline problems with secondary school children often stem from their desperate need to move, stretch and recharge their batteries after long periods of sitting. As language teachers we need to bear people's physical needs clearly in mind. In this section you will find plenty of useful exercises for teenagers.

Teaching adults between 8.00 PM and 10.00 PM can be an uphill grind, with you and the students drooping further and further into exhaustion. Ten minutes spent doing one of the exercises in this section can change the mood in the group and give them back their desire and ability to learn. There is no point in ignoring student fatigue and ploughing on through your lesson regardless.

We have used these energy raisers as warm-ups at the beginning of a lesson, as wake-up activities half way through and occasionally at the very end of a class to make sure people leave the group in an alert, happy frame of mind. Have fun!

## QUICK ENERGY RAISERS

### In class

- Have everyone in the class breathe in and out three times in unison.
- Have everyone breathe in through their left nostril and out through their right one and then vice versa. (Even if this doesn't work it'll make the students laugh, which will raise energy.)
- Clear away all the classroom furniture or go out and find a large space. Explain to the students that you are going to play tag, but instead of having to touch the other person anywhere they have to touch the other person's foot with their hand. This is rather robust, so allow anybody who doesn't want to participate to opt out. Make sure everyone looks after their own safety and play for a short time only.
- Ask the students to push their chairs into a very tight horseshoe shape and stand on their chair. Explain that the extreme left-hand chair is the beginning of January and the extreme right-hand chair is the end of December. The students are to rearrange themselves in the order in which their birthdays come in the year but without getting down off the chairs.

### RATIONALE

A couple of minutes spent on non-language activities like the first three above will pay dividends for the students in subsequent language work.

## 4.1

**LEVEL**
Beginner +

**TIME**
2–3 minutes

**MATERIALS**
None

**PREPARATION**
None

ACKNOWLEDGEMENT
We learnt foot tag from Meg Bond and the chair exercise from Judy Baker.

## 4.2

**LEVEL**
Beginner +

**TIME**
5–10 minutes

**MATERIALS**
None

**PREPARATION**
None

# WAVES

## In class

1 Put the furniture against the walls or go out of the classroom and find an open space. Ask the students to line up in two rows facing one another, as far apart as the space allows.
2 Explain that one line are the waters of the river coming down. The other line are the sea coming up the estuary. Get the two lines to advance *very* gently towards each other, with arms linked, until they meet in the centre of the space. The two lines gently touch and then flow back. Tell them the wind is rising and the waters now flow together a bit faster – they meet and move back.
3 Repeat this five to seven times with the movement forward and back gradually increasing in pace until by the end a storm is blowing and the waters crash together.

### RATIONALE

This exercise allows a sleepy group to shake off its lethargy and experience its own power. The power is always there – sometimes it just needs tapping.

ACKNOWLEDGEMENT
We learnt this technique from Marcia Karp, a psychodramatist.

## 4.3

**LEVEL**
Beginner +

**TIME**
5–10 minutes

**MATERIALS**
None

**PREPARATION**
None

# LOUD CONVERSATION

## In class

1 Put the furniture against the walls or go out of the classroom and find an open space. Ask the students to line up in two rows facing each other about a metre and a half apart. Each person should have a partner in the row facing.
2 Now ask the students to pick a new partner diagonally opposite them, two or three places along the opposite row. All the students have a conversation with their diagonal partners, simultaneously.

**RATIONALE**

The noise level automatically rises and people pick up energy from those around them.

ACKNOWLEDGEMENT

We learnt this exercise from André Fonck, a teacher with the Belgian Office de l'Emploi.

# RATS AND RABBITS

## In class

**4.4**

**LEVEL**
Beginner +

**TIME**
5–15 minutes

**MATERIALS**
None

**PREPARATION**
None

1 Move all the furniture to the back of the room to leave as much space as possible. Ask the students to make two rows, side by side, about a metre apart along the centre of the room. You stand at the head of the rows.

2 Since this is quite a rough activity, start by asking each student to take responsibility for their personal safety. Now explain that the left hand row are 'rats' and the right hand row are 'rabbits'. You are going to say *Rrrrr . . . rats* or *Rrrrr . . . rabbits.* If you say *Rats* the rats have to run and touch the wall nearest to them before they are touched by a rabbit and if you say *Rabbits*, the rabbits have to rush to their nearest wall before they are touched by a rat. If a student is touched they then have to join the other row.

3 When, after a minute or two, the students have got the idea of playing the game as 'rats' and 'rabbits', change the names of the teams using the variations listed below.

**VARIATIONS**

**Minimal pairs**  This activity can also be given a language focus. The teams are named 'pins' and 'pens'. You shout out either one of the words and the appropriate team has to try to reach the safety of their wall before they are touched. Every time they get on top of the sounds, rename the teams again – *bath/bathe, walk/work, think/sink*, etc.

**Wordstress**  The left-hand team is called 'first syllable stress', the right-hand one 'second syllable stress'. Example words: *fourteen/forty, police/palace*, etc.

**Right and wrong**  One team represents correct sentences, and the other wrong ones. Example sentences: *I will going to London, I've been to London yesterday*, etc. This works well with sentences taken from the students' homework.

**Meaningful and meaningless**   Example sentences: *The roof is open, The watch is dead, English is German and French, Teachers are going to be students, Everything has no meaning.*

### NOTE

This exercise can be done outside if you haven't got enough room in your class.

### ACKNOWLEDGEMENT

Paul learnt this exercise when he was a member of the Woodcraft Folk (a cooperative voluntary youth organisation) in the early sixties, but it's probably much older.

## 4.5

**LEVEL**
Elementary +

**TIME**
20–30 minutes

**MATERIALS**
None

**PREPARATION**
You need a room with tables out of the way and chairs in a big circle round the room

## FRUIT SALAD

## In class

1  All the students are seated in a circle with you standing in the middle. Ask each student to choose the name of a fruit. (It doesn't matter if some students choose the same one.) They should all say the fruit they have chosen loud and clear so that everyone hears.

2  Now say *I'd like a fruit salad with* . . . adding the names of a few of the fruits chosen. All the students whose fruits you have said change seats and you slip into a seat. This will leave one of the students stranded in the middle – 'it'. 'It' calls out another 'fruit salad' and tries to slip into a seat. Play the game in this simple form for a couple of minutes.

3  Ask the students to pair off. Their task will be to play the game again while observing their partner's strategy for getting a chair. Play for another three to four minutes. Ask the partners to comment to each other on what they noticed about the other's strategy.

4  In the last round of the game, ask each person to adopt their partner's strategy while continuing to observe their partner, who this time is trying to behave like them.

5  The partners come together to comment on what it felt like being the other and observing the other trying to be them.

### RATIONALE

This exercise combines energy-rousing movement and competition with mental concentration on the partner. If you ask people to do several things at once they will often discover energy and capacity they did not know they had.

### ACKNOWLEDGEMENT

We learnt this exercise from Joan Agosta (See Bibliography for details of published work).

# INDIVIDUALS, SUB-GROUPS AND GROUPS

## In class

1  Get the students sitting in a circle. Ask everyone who is, say, wearing earrings to get up and form a sub-group in the middle. Encourage them to stay in the middle for half a minute or so, maybe to put their arms around each others' shoulders and to exchange a few comments.
2  When the sub-group has split up, suggest more sub-groups that the students could form: everybody who has a cat, who hates writing, who is good at English, who doesn't like standing in the centre, who hasn't stood in the centre yet, etc.
3  After you've suggested a few categories, hand the exercise over to the students, getting them to suggest their own categories. Each time a group forms, encourage them to have a brief conversation and also encourage the students who are left sitting down to exchange comments.

### RATIONALE

If students have worked together in the same group for some time, tedium can develop. In this exercise they discover that they also belong to subsets within the group. A change plus plenty of movement and you have raised energy levels.

### VARIATIONS

Give everyone a minute or so and ask them to think of one thing which is true of them but of no one else in the room. Have everyone say what they thought of.

**4.6**

**LEVEL**
Elementary +

**TIME**
15–30 minutes

**MATERIALS**
None

**PREPARATION**
None

# MULTIPLE TASKS

## In class

1  Ask the students to work in pairs. They are going to have a five-minute conversation about anything they like. But one of them is going to take on a secondary task, which is to spend the first minute or so of the conversation maintaining eye contact with their partner. When they are satisfied that they are doing this they should then continue to maintain eye contact *and* observe what their partner is doing with their hands. If and when they feel they are doing both these tasks as well as maintaining the conversation, they should then observe their own hands as well.
2  When you have explained the exercise to the students, ask them to decide who is going to take on the extra tasks. Then ask them to start the conversation, explaining that you will time them.

**4.7**

**LEVEL**
Elementary +

**TIME**
5 minutes

**MATERIALS**
None

**PREPARATION**
None

3 The primary aim of this exercise is to establish rapport between the students. You could then, however, go into the process of the exercise by asking them, say, how it felt different from a normal conversation or how well they did the observation tasks. This exercise is also a good cue for a discussion on eye contact and body language.

### RATIONALE

In this exercise, the students are asked to do up to four things simultaneously: converse, maintain eye contact, watch the other person's hands, watch their own. If people are tired, asking them to do a lot more than they would normally do will often draw them out of their low energy state and leave them revitalised.

### ACKNOWLEDGEMENT

This exercise is taken from *The Structure of Magic* (Bandler and Grinder 1975).

## 4.8

**LEVEL**
Lower
intermediate +

**TIME**
10–20 minutes

**MATERIALS**
None

**PREPARATION**
Be ready to tell an
anecdote/story

# STOPPING THE STORY-TELLER

## In class

1 Explain to the group that you are going to try and tell a story – they are to stop you by asking as many questions as they can about the story. You must answer each question and try and keep the narrative moving at the same time!
2 For homework, ask three or four students to come ready to tell stories of their own.
3 In the next lesson, have two or three people tell their stories to half or a third of the class. The listeners' task is the same as it was during your telling.

### RATIONALE

This technique provokes higher energy levels – voices rise. If the questioning really gets going as a fast game, a lot of aggression is let out playfully, and the story-teller's adrenalin flows. Some colleagues are tempted to use the technique as a group revenge mechanism by picking story-tellers from among the most dominant students in the group. This can be dangerous.

### ACKNOWLEDGEMENT

We learnt this idea from André Fonck who works for L'Office de l'Emploi in Belgium.

# CHAPTER 5

# *Giving students control*

This is perhaps the most complex and challenging section of the book, as the basic proposal is the democratisation of the classroom, a social system very close to the authoritarian family or to a monarchical system. *Student planning commitees* (p. 56) suggests the handing over of course planning to the student group, while *Negotiating discipline* (p. 55) proposes that the group decide for itself what its behavioural norms should be.

The complexity lies in the students' individual, competing needs and the difficulty of sensitive inter-student negotiation. Just how different learners are from one another becomes clear if you do the exercises on *Sharing learning rhythms* (p. 59), and *The brilliance of one's own process* (p. 58).

In many ways, turning over the planning of the course content to students is still a fairly superficial transfer of power as so many hidden things go on in a group in which people sit and move and work together. Exercises like *Peer opinions* (p. 68) and *What do they want from me?* (p. 66) are an attempt to get students to become more aware of some of these under-the-surface processes.

A very useful book to read in parallel with trying some of these exercises is *Freedom to learn for the Eighties* (Rogers 1983).

## STUDENTS' RIGHTS QUESTIONNAIRE

### In class

1 Pre-teach any vocabulary the students may not know, photocopy and give out the questionnaire on the next page.
2 Ask each person to read the items and tick the appropriate boxes. Every fifth item is blank. Ask the students to fill in an assertion or a right.
3 Group the students in threes or fours to compare their feelings about these statements.

**5.1**

**LEVEL**
Intermediate +

**TIME**
30–45 minutes

**MATERIALS**
One copy each of the Students' rights questionnaire

**PREPARATION**
None

## Students' rights questionnaire

| A = STRONGLY AGREE   B = AGREE   C = NEUTRAL<br>D = DISAGREE   E = STRONGLY DISAGREE | A | B | C | D | E |
|---|---|---|---|---|---|
| 1    I have the right to have forgotten things. | | | | | |
| 2    I have the right to insist that I get what I pay for. | | | | | |
| 3    I have the right to demand translations into my mother tongue. | | | | | |
| 4    I have the right to make mistakes. | | | | | |
| 5 | | | | | |
| 6    I have the right to ask English speakers to respect my culture. | | | | | |
| 7    I have the right to spend some time each day as I wish. | | | | | |
| 8    I have the right to choose my teachers. | | | | | |
| 9    I have the right to *my* way of pronouncing English. | | | | | |
| 10 | | | | | |
| 11   I have the right to come to class late, or not to come. | | | | | |
| 12   I have the right to be heard when I want to say something. | | | | | |
| 13   I have the right to choose which level class I am in. | | | | | |
| 14   I have the right to tell others what I am feeling. | | | | | |
| 15 | | | | | |
| 16   I have the right to my own space, on which no one may impinge. | | | | | |
| 17   I have the right to use any kind of dictionary I want. | | | | | |
| 18   I have the right to an explanation of any action that affects me. | | | | | |
| 19   I have a right both to do and not to do homework. | | | | | |
| 20 | | | | | |
| 21   I have the right to set my own priorities. | | | | | |
| 22   I have the right to say *No* to requests without having to explain. | | | | | |
| 23   I have the right not to know things the teacher has taught me. | | | | | |
| 24   I have the right to be treated differently from other students. | | | | | |
| 25 | | | | | |

# NEGOTIATING DISCIPLINE
## In class

**5.2**

**LEVEL**
Beginner +

**TIME**
15–30 minutes

**MATERIALS**
None

**PREPARATION**
None

1 Over the first ten to twenty hours of a course, a number of discipline problems often come up. Some we have noticed are:
 - lack of punctuality
 - problems over who sits near whom
 - yawning, stretching, fidgeting to show boredom, restlessess, etc.
 - absenteeism
 - rude use of the mother tongue (in multinational classes)
 - use of dictionaries the teacher considers inefficient, etc.

 List the discipline problems you have noted in your class, with the help of the students. Tell them you are going to leave them for a few minutes to allow them time to decide how these should be sorted out. Tell them to call you back when they have reached their decisions.
2 Offer the group a free-of-you negotiating session whenever there seems to be a need for this.
3 Following a group decision, you and the group have to abide by it. As teacher, you enforce such decisions until such time as there is a further group decision to change the rule.

## RATIONALE

Giving students control of what, how, when and why they do something is an obvious way of increasing their confidence. People who complain of 'sick building syndrome' speak of having no air, no light, of it being too hot, etc but more importantly they mention lack of control – being free to open a window is more important to a student than hyper-modern air-conditioning and may prevent a build-up of frustration. For example, before handing over responsibility for discipline to the group, I used to spend a lot of time and energy coaxing, training and finally forcing students to use English-English dictionaries. The first time I handed this decision over to them, the group decided to use translation dictionaries for the first month of the three-month course and then all to use English dictionaries. At the beginning of the second month they changed the previous decision: people could use either sort of diction-ary as they wished. At that time I felt their second decision was a wrong one, but I had to accept it. If you don't want to obey group decisions then don't offer the students the power to negotiate rules.

## 5.3

**LEVEL**
Beginner +

**TIME**
15–45 minutes

**MATERIALS**
None

**PREPARATION**
None

# STUDENT PLANNING COMMITTEES

## In class

1 Offer the class the best, most appropriate and varied programme you can for the first hours of the course. The group need to know what you are capable of. At a symbolically suitable moment (the end of the first week on an intensive UK course, at the end of the first month in a system like the German adult education system where students have a lesson once or twice a week) announce that, at their next meeting, the group will become an executive committee or Student Planning Committee (SPC): They will review the work done so far and decide how they want the programme changed over the next week/month.

2 On the day of the SPC, tell the group you will leave them to their deliberations for between fifteen and thirty minutes. They should come and get you when they are ready. You will want clear instructions for the following week/month when they call you back into the classroom. They are to consider both content and methodology.

3 When you are recalled, take notes on the group's decisions.

For example, there were twelve people in my upper-intermediate UK group. For four of them this was their sixth SPC, for eight it was their second time. Two of the learners were in their forties while the rest were of university student age and background.

The decisions the group took were for the five classes the following week:

■ Please continue with the interviews with native-speakers in which we take notes on special expressions and words they use – two mornings.

■ Please drop the grammar book we have used for the last two weeks We need grammar but use other exercises or another book.

■ The story-writing last week was good – one morning on that again.

■ You are free to offer us what you decide on the fifth morning.

This group gave me a clear plan for the following week – it took them fifteen minutes. They had decided on their own content and, in part, on the methodology to be used. The process was clear, public and contractual.

### PROBLEMS OF INTRODUCING SPC's

When the teacher first proposes the system, most students do not believe their decisions will be loyally implemented. SPC's can be dominated by one or two vociferous students. Many teachers experience fear when introduced to the idea of SPC's:

■ fear of being got at

■ fear of being forced to do things they don't want to

■ fear of the change of rapport with the students that SPC's entail
  However, if real in spirit and letter, SPC's offer a revolution in classroom relationships. The students become joint organisers of the work done. They achieve a staffroom relationship with the teacher.

This proposal conflicts with the great bulk of most students' previous educational experience.

Sue Leather (Director of Studies at Cambridge Academy of English) writes about her problems introducing SPC's.

Although I had been teaching for a number of years, I had never really successfully managed to get 'uncoloured' feedback from my students. I now realise that this was because I had never thought into the dynamics properly. I had many stabs at it: the usual things – suggestion boxes, grammar points on the wall, even asking students directly what they enjoyed, and why. It is easy to kid yourself that you are asking for feedback and for suggestions, when all the time you are really protecting yourself from these very things. Not only that, but students also have their own camouflage . . .

Using the *crítica de cátedra** was a definite move in the right direction. There are two aspects to it for me: 1) technical, and 2) attitudinal; aspects which are very much interlinked.

The most important technical points are that:

a The students can organise their own discussion once given guidelines, e.g. 'We want a critique of this week and marching orders for next week'.

b Two teachers working together is better than one alone – it prevents students from game-playing and encourages an adult – adult interaction.

c You avoid getting involved in the discussion stage, even through eye-contact.

The attitudinal area, though absolutely fundamental, is more difficult to describe, and certainly more difficult to achieve:

a You are totally open to criticism – this implies trust, since you must feel that they will not be unkind or tactless, at least not purposefully.

b You do not react to criticism or suggestions either by open hostility/ rejection or by showing approval (this is more difficult than it sounds!). You *do* thank them for their comments, and show that you appreciate their help.

c You *act upon* their suggestions.

Although I do not fool myself that my students always feel they can say exactly what they would like to, I do feel that they have gained confidence in the validity of their own judgements. They have certainly become progressively bolder in their requests! I have gained the confidence of knowing that I am no less a teacher for hearing the criticisms of my students or for knowing that I will not react badly to their suggestions.

* The first time we know of SPC's being used was in Córdoba, Argentina in 1917. The term used there was *crítica de cátedra*.

**SPC's IN SECONDARY EDUCATION**

We know of concrete examples in the Canaries and in Denmark where planning the work ahead has been successfully negotiated with secondary school learners.

## 5.4

**LEVEL**
Lower
intermediate +

**TIME**
45 minutes

**MATERIALS**
Six or seven copies of
a page with six short
varied texts on it, to
cater for different
tastes

**PREPARATION**
None

# THE BRILLIANCE OF ONE'S OWN PROCESS

## In class

1  Put up the copies of the texts in the corridor outside your classroom. Ask the students to go outside and choose two or three passages they like. They are then to transcribe them *in the classroom*. They can make as many journeys as they like between the corridor and the classroom. They may not take writing materials into the corridor. While this is going on, observe how people read, walk and write.

2  At the end of the transcription exercise, when people have checked their texts with the texts on the walls, tell them some of the things you have observed about the way they read, walked and wrote. Explain that this is what is outwardly observable, but that you would like to find out what each person's inner process was.

3  In the process discussion, people tend to use very vague language like *I read the text and memorised it.* Ask the speaker to make words like *memorise* more precise. *Did you see it with your mind's eye or hear it with you mind's ear? Did you mumble the text as you walked? Did your way of doing the task change as the exercise went on? Was your way of walking affected by the rhythm of the sentence you were mentally carrying?* etc. The best way of running the discussion is to get one student to describe their process in some detail and then to get someone with a very different process to speak. Many people seem to expect that everybody will have done the task the same way as them, so realising the differences can become quite exciting. The whole point of this activity is to become aware of how thrillingly different people are from one another and that there are umpteen 'right' ways.

**VARIATIONS**

1  The idea of a process discussion can be applied to any activity. Ask each student to write a five-sentence story including these key words: *tree, child, goat.* In small groups they read the stories to each other. Then ask them to be specific about the process of the writing. This could involve expressing some of the ideas that did not go into the story, how they built the five sentences up, the side thoughts they had as they wrote, doubts about language, etc. Sometimes you achieve a greater respect for other people when you realise how originally different they are from you.

**2** During his last Bristol seminar, Caleb Gattegno asked the trainee group to take the word *signature* and see how many other words they could make with the letters in the word, e.g. *nag, gnat, sign, nature,* etc. He gave us about seven minutes for the task and then asked us to make explicit the mental processes we had been through. As you would expect, there was a fascinating variety. This workshop was in Autumn 1987 and Dr Gattegno died in July 1988.

# SHARING LEARNING RHYTHMS
## In class

This exercise is useful some way into a course, two thirds of the way through a course or at the end of a course.

**1** Ask each student to draw a graph. The horizontal axis represents the time from the start of the course until now. The vertical axis represents the intensity and quantity of the student's learning.

**2** Ask students to get together in groups of six to eight and compare their learning graphs. It may be worth highlighting certain graphs on the board for the whole group to look at. In our experience students are often amazed at other people's rhythms and frequently take heart from hearing about them.

In a UK language school an Italian student came up with the graph in Fig. 6 at the end of a month's study. The graph in Fig. 7 was produced by a twelve-week-stay student from Turkey.

Başak, from Turkey, explained that she had almost given up about two thirds of the way through her course until, one day, she just decided to pull her socks up and start making an effort to learn again. This greatly cheered up the Italian who felt that her own learning curve over the previous ten days had been steadily downwards.

In this case, the sharing of rhythms offered a saddened student a new and better way of looking at her feelings. Sometimes a student's graph

**5.5**

**LEVEL**
Beginner +

**TIME**
40 minutes

**MATERIALS**
None

**PREPARATION**
None

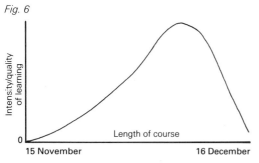

*Fig. 6*

Intensity/quality of learning

Length of course

15 November          16 December

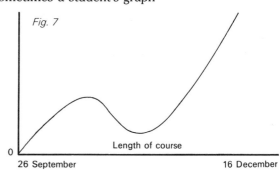

*Fig. 7*

Length of course

26 September          16 December

suggests a pattern that applies to many people in the group, as with the nine month graph in Fig. 8 (the dashed lines on the graph represent short holidays).

This student said: *For the first three months I studied hard. I took the exam in June. During the term I was not aware of any special progress. When I came back at the end of June, I knew I had improved. I felt the same after my September holiday.*

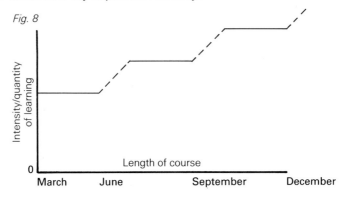

Fig. 8

## 5.6 EXAGGERATING CULTURAL STEREOTYPES

### In class

**LEVEL**
Beginner +; relevant to students studying in an English-speaking country

**TIME**
15–30 minutes

**MATERIALS**
None

**PREPARATION**
None

1 Once students have been in an English-speaking country for a couple of weeks, ask each of them to jot down ten 'stupid questions' about their culture that they get asked again and again by foreign people. Ask the students to form small groups to share the questions.

2 Open up a discussion on how people cope with and parry the stereotypes that the questions imply. One of our Turkish students got fed up with Spanish students in the school asking him: *Do you have cars in Turkey or do you still ride on camels?* His response was to humorously inflate the Turkish stereotype: *No, we don't really like driving cars. My family lives in downtown Istanbul and my father has a stable with 100 camels in it. Each summer we ride the camels across the desert to Mecca. If my father can't get enough time off from his business, then we take a magic carpet!*

You are likely to find that quite a number of students have evolved equally ingenious ways of rebutting stupid projections on them and their culture.

### RATIONALE

Living in a foreign culture and speaking the foreign language for most of the day is a considerable strain for some people. The language classroom is the natural place to let off steam about the oddness, hostility and racism of the host society. Openly dealing with this tangentially deals with the similar hostilities between the national and racial groups within the school, e.g. Arabs and Israelis, Chinese and Japanese, etc.

# CHANGE OF VIEWPOINT
## In class

1 Have everyone sit alone. Ask each member of the group to choose one aspect of their present learning situation they are unhappy with or that they know can be improved. Ask them to bring this aspect to mind and think of a few examples.

2 Write the following sentences on the board and ask each person to complete the sentences. Make sure that everyone understands that what they write will be confidential unless they wish to reveal it.

It's difficult for me to _____
I'm going to try to _____
I can't _____
One day I'll _____
I'd like to _____
I can't stand _____

3 When each person in the group has finished, give them a few moments to consider what they have written. Then give them the following alternative beginnings:

It's a challenge for me to _____
I'm going to _____
I'm sure that _____
Soon I'll _____
I know that I can _____
I won't stand _____

4 Ask the group to rewrite their original sentences with the above beginnings. When they have finished, make it clear that they can amend any sentences which do not work for them or for the grammar of English.

5 Finally ask how people feel. People will generally say they feel much better and most people will want to talk about their thoughts in a positive way.

This exercise can be used equally validly with a teacher development group. I did this exercise on a day I was feeling very negative (not to say racist) about a group of students. My sentences were as follows:

**5.7**

**LEVEL**
Intermediate +

**TIME**
30–45 minutes

**MATERIALS**
None

**PREPARATION**
None

It's difficult for me to understand Swiss.
I'm going to try to educate them.
I can't seem to like them.
One day I'll get to the bottom of this.
I'd like to be interested in them.
I can't stand them talking about money.

They became:
It's a challenge for me to understand Swiss.
I'm going to educate them.
I'm sure I'll (get) to like them.
Soon I'll get to the bottom of this.
I know that I can be interested in them.
I won't stand them talking about money.

I felt better!

ACKNOWLEDGEMENT
We learnt this technique from John Syer and Christopher Connolly. They acknowledge the Esalen Institute of California as their source.

# 5.8

## CREATING A GOOD ATMOSPHERE

**LEVEL**
Elementary +

**TIME**
30 minutes

**MATERIALS**
None

**PREPARATION**
Be prepared to tell a story to the group

### BEFORE CLASS

Bring to mind a success story of yours. It can be something very minor like solving a small technical problem or it could be a major life success. Be ready to tell it to the group.

## In class

Tell the group your success story. Give them some thinking time and ask them to come up with success stories of their own. Find out how many people have such stories ready to tell. Ask these people to work in small groups with people who have not yet thought of any. Don't pressurise the people who can't recall success stories fast. Once the small groups get going, many students who could not at first remember stories find them coming.

### RATIONALE

Even for students who don't like studying languages, it is warming to be asked to speak of their successes in other fields. Focussing on pleasurable things may make even the language class seem more palatable.

### NOTES

For a few students, being asked to think about successes brings failures to mind. This is a risk you have to take.

# WHAT ARE YOU FEELING NOW?

## In class

1 Ask each person to think of one adjective to describe exactly how· they are feeling right now. They may need to use dictionaries. They should not tell their adjective to people round them. Once everybody has got an adjective, everybody stands up.
2 Say a few adjectives, e.g. *sleepy, angry, sad, excited,* etc. The students sit down as soon as you hit their adjective. When half the students have sat down, stop calling out adjectives yourself and ask the seated students to take over the adjective calling.

### RATIONALE

It is a sign of confidence when students are willing to say how they feel at a given moment. Sometimes just the saying will lighten a bad mood in a group.

### VARIATIONS

You can use the same exercise frame with different content.

**Telling the time:** Students sit down when you shout out the time they got up (*twenty-five to six/twenty to six/a quarter to six,* etc.)

**Gerunds:** Students sit down when you have called out something they once wanted to do but never got round to doing (*cross-country skiing/ skin-diving/learning the violin,* etc.).

**Names:** Students choose an adjective which starts with the same first letter as their first name. This is a good way of check that everyone knows each other's names a few days after a course has started.

ACKNOWLEDGEMENT
We learnt this exercise at a psychodrama workshop led by Barbara Tregear.

**5.9**

**LEVEL**
Post-beginner +

**TIME**
5–15 minutes

**MATERIALS**
None

**PREPARATION**
None

# CONGRATULATIONS

## In class

1 If the level of the group requires it, pre-teach *I congratulate you on . . . -ing* or other noun phrase.
2 If possible, get the group sitting or standing in a circle. Congratulate a couple of people on something about them. Get them to acknowledge the congratulation by thanking you with eye contact. People then congratulate each other round the circle and acknowledge. To some the exercise will seem strange at first and you may have to cope with some giggling.

The same technique can be used with a colleague group in the context

**5.10**

**LEVEL**
Post-beginner +

**TIME**
10 minutes

**MATERIALS**
None

**PREPARATION**
None

of a staff meeting or a teacher development group meeting. What follows is Katie Head's description of this exercise being used among teachers at the Cambridge Eurocentre in the context of a development group:

Morale has been very low this term. I've been suffering a bit myself – feeling I wasn't coping with the job as well as I usually do. For all kinds of reasons, people are not feeling good about their work. There's an 'atmosphere' about the place.

We have decided to talk about morale this week in our Teacher Development session. Janie came, she's one of our supply teachers, and she happened to be around. There were eight of us in the group. It was Janie who started us off. She said, 'Why don't we begin by going round the circle and each saying one thing we've done this week which has made us feel good?'

It was surprisingly difficult, at the end of a day's work in an atmosphere of low morale, to cast the mind in such a positive direction, but each of us in turn managed to focus on something that had brightened the week, even if it was only washing the kitchen floor! Already I felt better.

'Now,' Janie continued to take control. Jokingly she warned us we might not find the next activity very easy. 'What I think we should do now is go round and say something nice about every other person in the group. Pay a compliment to each of your colleagues. And – this is very important – accept your compliments without embarrassment; don't get uncomfortable just because people are saying nice things about you.'

People were hesitant. I was intrigued, curious, a little uneasy. We took time to think about what we wanted to say. After a pause, Heather volunteered to kick off. I don't remember what she said about me, but I know it was something nice, generous, and above all genuinely meant; and it made me feel good about my role in the school.

We each took our turn; nobody was compelled to speak, but most wanted to. I felt good about what the other teachers said about me. I felt even better about being able to tell each of them how and why I appreciated them. In just a few minutes the mood of the group had changed completely. We had arrived tired, tense, pressured; now people were listening, sharing, supporting and affirming each other's strengths and qualities, as colleagues and teachers working together for the school.

When the bell rang at 4.15, we retired to the staff room. Usually people can't wait to get away at the end of the day, but today they stayed around. The mood was relaxed, supportive, optimistic. We had created a momentum which drew others into its orbit. Ideas were flying around, people were talking positively about their work, about the school, about themselves.

We could have spent the Development session voicing a list of grievances that are contributing to the low morale in the school.

Instead we found a way as individuals to break out of the prevailing mood of despondency and focus on the better side of everybody's job. Is it just wishful thinking, or can we all learn to give each other the occasional pat on the back? It really does do wonders to raise morale.

**NOTE**

The experiences of the Cambridge Eurocentre Teacher Development group are documented in *Development for Teachers not Trainers* (Rees Miller forthcoming).

## GUESSING HIDDEN STRENGTHS

### In class

1 Ask each student to write one sentence like this: *I am good at . . . -ing.* Tell them to choose a hidden strength that most others in the group do not know about.
2 Divide the class into two teams and collect all the sentences. Read them out twice. Each group then picks a sentence they think was written by a person in the other team. If Team A are right in their matching of sentence to person, then that person joins their team. Team A then has another guess. If Team A guesses wrong then their round is over and Team B starts guessing. The aim of the game is to capture all the opposing team. No one is allowed to reveal their sentence until it is correctly guessed.

**RATIONALE**

In some cultures it is quite hard to say good things about yourself – it feels arrogant and embarrassing. In the exercise the self-assertion is disguised by the competitive team-game frame.

ACKNOWLEDGEMENT
We learnt this exercise from Maggie Rotherham who herself learnt it from a student.

**5.11**

**LEVEL**
Elementary +

**TIME**
20–30 minutes

**MATERIALS**
None

**PREPARATION**
None

## 5.12

**LEVEL**
Elementary +

**TIME**
15–30 minutes

**MATERIALS**
None

**PREPARATION**
None

# SAY IT NOW

## In class

1 At the end of a week, a month or any reasonable part of a course, suggest to the students there are plenty of things we want to say but do not manage to say when we want to. This is the time to share some of the things they did not say earlier in the course. Set the ball rolling by telling them three or four things you have held back.

2 Ask people to write down two or three sentences each. They read out their sentences and explain about when they had wanted to say them.

For example, in an upper-intermediate class in the UK, Mario told the group:

- This class is like being on holiday for me, especially after my beginners' class.
- Sonia's absences from class annoy me – illogically I also feel annoyed when she comes to class.
- I don't like this room stuck up in an attic.

### VARIATIONS

For students studying in the UK it can be quite a relief to share in class some of the things they have wanted to say in their host families, but which they did not manage to say.

In a teacher development group we have found people needing to give open vent to feelings they had held back in a previous staff meeting or union meeting. *Say it now* can be a real safety valve.

## 5.13

**LEVEL**
Lower
intermediate +

**TIME**
30–60 minutes

**MATERIALS**
Two sheets of paper
for each student

**PREPARATION**
None

# WHAT DO THEY WANT FROM ME?

## In class

1 Organise the class into sub-groups of ten to fifteen students. Each student takes a sheet of paper and lists the names of the people in their sub-group down the left-hand side. To the right of the names they rule three columns with the headings below (see Fig. 9).

| What I want from them | | | |
|---|---|---|---|
| Name | More | Less | No change |
| | | | |

Fig. 9

2 Ask the students each to write a word or a phrase expressing what they would like *more of, less of* or areas in which they want *no change* from a given classmate (see Fig. 10).

| Levent | clear ideas | smoking | his enthusiasm |

Fig. 10

Each student writes such comments against the names of every other person in their sub-group.

3 In preparation for the communicative phase of the exercise each student prepares a second sheet. The heading this time is 'What they want from me' (see Fig. 11).

| What they want from me | | | |
|---|---|---|---|
| Name | More | Less | No change |
| Levent wants Giovanna wants | | | |

Fig. 11

4 The students now move around within their sub-group, pairing off with each person in turn. They find out what each person wants from them and note it down on their second sheet (see above). Encourage them to take as much time as they need on these exchanges. Also allow time for people to go back and talk to the same people again once their 'What they want from me' sheets have been completed.

## RATIONALE

Confidence includes noticing and coming to terms with other people's positive and negative feelings about you. This exercise is a mechanism for allowing this to happen. How honest and open the exchange can be depends on the mood and development of the group. There are some groups we would not use this exercise with.

ACKNOWLEDGEMENT
The exercise, originally called *Role Negotiation,* was invented by Roger Harrison – we came across it in *The Red Book of Groups* (Houston 1984).

## 5.14

**LEVEL**
Elementary +

**TIME**
60–90 minutes

**MATERIALS**
One copy each of the
Peer opinions grid

**PREPARATION**
None

# PEER OPINIONS

## In class

1 Split the class into groups of twelve to fifteen people. Photocopy and give out the Peer opinions grid on the opposite page and ask people to put their own name at the top and the names of all the people in their sub-group down the left-hand side. They then fill in the 'praise' column and the 'needs to' column for each of the people in the sub-group.

2 Once most people have filled in the grids, each sub-group chooses one of its members and everybody else reads out what they have written about them. Encourage the students to explain and elaborate on what they have written. Ask the student in the 'hot-seat' to acknowledge each comment rather than cringing and going under the table. Allow them to react to their group's comments as a whole.

3 Don't forget to let the whole class read out their comments on you. Acknowledge each one, *including* the positive ones.

### RATIONALE

A mark of confidence is that you can accept praise both internally and in a social context. The same goes for criticism. People from different cultures have very different norms in this area and a good follow-up to this exercise is to leave time for discussion of praise-giving and blaming rules in the students' culture/s and in the target culture.

## Peer opinions grid

| Name | | |
| --- | --- | --- |
| Name | She or he is good at English because . . . | She or he needs to . . . |
| 1 | | |
| 2 | | |
| 3 | | |
| 4 | | |
| 5 | | |
| 6 | | |
| 7 | | |
| 8 | | |
| 9 | | |
| 10 | | |
| 11 | | |
| 12 | | |
| 13 | | |
| 14 | | |
| 15 | | |

The teacher is good at teaching because _____
_____
She or he needs to _____
_____

## 5.15  END-OF-COURSE FEEDBACK

Feedback by questionnaire is easily quantifiable but it is cold, dead and static compared to the more interactive ways outlined below.

### ANONYMOUS FEEDBACK

The teacher gives each student a slip of paper. They ask each person to write down three positive things about the course and three negative ones. Students are asked to write clearly and not to write their names.

The papers are collected, shuffled and given out again. No one should have their own paper. The papers are read out; anyone may comment on what is read, except for the reader, who symbolically represents the person who wrote the thoughts.

An administrative advantage of this system is that the slips can be collected and evaluated beyond the classroom.

### STUDENTS DECIDE THE FEEDBACK CATEGORIES

The teacher and the class group brainstorm the categories under which feedback should be collected. Each category heading is written on a large sheet of paper. The papers are placed on tables round the room. Students walk round the room and write their comments under the headings decided by the group. The sheets are read out to the whole group.

### SECRET INDIVIDUAL FEEDBACK

Students may feel a need to say particular things to particular people without these things being made public. They may want private communication with the teacher. The teacher gives out several sheets of paper to each student and suggests they write their feedback thoughts to appropriate people in the group. They may also write 'letters for publication' that are posted on the walls of the room. As soon as a letter is written it is either posted or delivered to its addressee. People receiving feedback letters are of course free to reply.

### LETTERS TO YOURSELF

The teacher brings letter paper and envelopes to the feedback session. Each student writes a letter to themself about their feelings and the course. They address the letter to their home and give the sealed envelope to the teacher for dispatch.

This feedback technique works on the correct notion that people only really know what they have learnt on a language course sometime after it is over. To receive a letter from oneself, written on the last day of the course, will sometimes help with this post-course internal evaluation.

### LEARNER-PROCESS EVALUATION

The teacher asks the students to come to this last session ready to describe their learning process over the period of study. A good starter is to ask them to draw a graph which plots two things: intensity of learning, and well-being/happiness. The teacher's task in this process description session is attentive listening. Comments are not useful. The focus is on the learner as protagonist, not on the teaching, that for some may be incidental.

## ORAL FEEDBACK CIRCLE

The students sit in a tight circle so that everybody can see everybody else. The teacher asks for feedback on the course and explains that they will not give theirs until everybody has spoken. The teacher's task is simply to listen openly and to take it in. They pass neither verbal, facial nor gestural comments on what the students tell them.

Paul wrote this about his experience of the *Oral feedback circle:*

I first did this exercise as the last hour of a twelve-hour confidence-building option*. At the beginning of the lesson I asked for a bit of feedback from the students (I really wanted it because I wasn't sure how the course had gone and what changes I needed to make if I was going to do it again). A few of the more confident ones said what they thought and there was then a long, pregnant pause. It was a difficult and uncomfortable silence of the kind that people rush to fill. A student asked me what I thought. Being a teacher I like the sound of my voice, but for some reason on this occasion (probably because I really wanted feedback and was interested in what everybody had to say) I said I'd say what I had to say only after everyone had spoken. I meant it seriously and the students took it seriously – there was a bit of panic from the quieter students and a return to the uncomfortableness of having a silence. A few more students spoke and a few who had already spoken elaborated or added to what they had already said (at least partly because they, personally, needed to fill the silence but also, I think, to protect the students who hadn't spoken).

Finally, we were down to three students who hadn't spoken. By now the discomfort had evaporated and the students who spoke to fill the silence had stopped speaking. Two were gently pressurised by the completeness of the silence into speaking. There was then a long pause before the last student said, 'I know the students in this class better than I know the students in my own class'*. The remaining bit of tension evaporated and I then went on to say some positive things about the class. The last student comment was genuine and, I think, not meant to be positive but I think it was one of the best compliments I've ever had from a student.

* These students were on an intensive course in Cambridge, UK. They had optional classes in the afternoons and this group had chosen a twelve-hour mini-course on confidence building. Hence comments like: *I know the students in this class better than I know the students in my own class.*

ACKNOWLEDGEMENTS
We learnt the 'Students decide the feedback categories' technique from Tessa Woodward. The 'Secret individual feedback' technique was from Mike Gradwell and Krys Markowski.

## 5.16

**LEVEL**
Lower intermediate +; relevant at the end of courses away from home

**TIME**
20–40 minutes

**MATERIALS**
None

# CONFIDENCE TO GO HOME
## Preparation

### BEFORE CLASS

Think of times you have been away from your home place. When you get back, there are probably people you suddenly see again who make you know you are really back. These people are often apparently 'secondary' people, like caretakers, local shop folk and others strongly associated with place. A 'marker' person for one of our German students was a man she saw through the window each morning pulling his cart to his allotment.

## In class

1 Tell the class about three or four people who make you realise you are back home after a journey.
2 Ask them to work in groups of six to eight and to tell each other of such people in their lives. (Some will talk about sights, sounds and smells rather than people.) Remind them they will be home in a short while.

### RATIONALE

For some people bridges and transitions are hard. This exercise draws on the power of the group to smooth the transition. For people who have come to depend a lot on the group it allows them to prepare for its finishing.

ACKNOWLEDGEMENT
We learnt the idea of local people making places real from Sophie Rinvolucri.

# CHAPTER 6

# *Interventions that have worked*

Through the rest of the book we have offered you schemes of action, lesson plans and recipes. This chapter is historical and deals with specific problems in student/group, student/teacher or teacher/teacher relationships. The problems are so specific that it may not always be possible to generalise out from them and thus offer schemes of action for other days and other places.

Many of the interventions that follow are based on the personal experience of the authors. And, as such, they are also a good example of the personal development that is possible within a teacher development group. A support group of the type we belonged to enabled us to put these problems on the table and reduce our isolation as teachers. Historically, each of the problems outlined in this section had a particular outcome.

The teacher development group we attended more than repaid the time we spent each week. We were able to talk over the type of problems we encountered in our day-to-day teaching in a supportive environment, get advice and often go away feeling energised and confident. Teachers need their confidence supporting as much as students.

## 6.1 A STAFFROOM DISCUSSION IN CLASS

### SITUATION

Paul Davis and Katie Plumb (Both teaching at Eurocentre, Cambridge) got into a staffroom discussion on how to present the future forms in English. Katie felt her definition of the forms was different from Paul's.

### CONTINUATION

They decided to continue their discussion of future forms in Katie's lower intermediate class. Here are their accounts of the event:

### PAUL'S VERSION

Katie has the future as a theme this week. On Tuesday morning, first lesson, Katie and I go into her class and sit near each other at the teacher's desk. None of the class know me (except one) but they know and like Katie. Katie gives minimal instructions. 'Paul and I are going to discuss the future, can you listen?' We spend fifteen minutes talking about the future; Katie's a bit artificial at first but only for the first couple of minutes. We meander on, saying what we think, sometimes disagreeing quite a lot – like a normal staff room coffee break discussion. We're unselfconscious after the first two minutes – we pretty much ignore the students – they do not ask questions (although there's no reason why they shouldn't). After fifteen minutes we turn towards the students who immediately jump in. Students say things – I disagree with them sometimes, listen to others, generally treat them as I did Katie. She doesn't intervene. After a few more minutes Katie indicates something to me, I whisper, 'Shall I go?' – she says, 'Yes.' I get up and say, 'Bye' – very warm student 'Thank you – Byeee'.

Katie said she had an excellent, buzzing, student discussion which went beyond what she and I had discussed. She then followed up by presenting *my* future worksheet (she disagreed with it) and they did this in relation to our and their discussion and Katie's slight disagreement with material presented.

## KATIE'S VERSION

I told my class that Paul was coming in but I didn't tell them why. When he came in I told them they could do whatever they liked; ignore us, listen, interrupt, etc. We then started to discuss the different future forms and the students followed our conversation. In the end, I think one of them asked us a question so we started to include them. When Paul left they wanted to know which tense it was that we had said wasn't important for them at their level (that was what they found most memorable).

I then asked them to clarify what we'd said because I was totally confused. I was amazed that they'd picked up on almost everything. I then gave them a matching exercise where they had to match the future tense form with the appropriate definition.

I felt quite nervous when Paul came into the class because I didn't know how the students would react. As it was a success I think I'll try it again (as long as it's a genuine discussion).

Paul also wrote these later impressions:

a  It's a good way of team teaching if you only have fifteen minutes to spare.

b  We treated the students like adults. In effect they were overhearing a teacher-to-teacher staffroom conversation. They responded accordingly.

c  Global presentation – all complexities up to and including the fact that two professional teachers didn't agree are dealt with. The students didn't bat an eyelid.

d  I'd like to do this again because we got such a good reaction from the students and because I like working with Katie.

## VARIATIONS

The format of two teachers having an open discussion in front of a class that one or both of them teach can be used for many purposes:

- Public debriefing: the class teacher talks through the past week's work with their colleague. The students are gradually drawn in and a feedback discussion develops. The colleague slips out and the discussion continues.
- Experiences from other classes that are relevant to this one: the two teachers bring up previous teaching experiences chosen for their potential relevance to the work in this class.
- Lesson planning: the two teachers brainstorm ideas for possible future lessons with the group, giving their reasons.

ACKNOWLEDGEMENT

These variations were suggested by John Morgan (See Bibliography for details of published work).


# 6.2 A STUDENT INTERVENTION THAT WORKED

## SITUATION

Paul Davis was fourteen. He arrived late for assembly. The normal pattern was for late-comers to join the non-Christians in a side-room and wait until prayers were over. Paul breezed down the main aisle of the school hall, greeting his mates. They giggled behind their hands – he had not noticed the whole school was at prayer. At the end of assembly the head announced he wanted to see Davis in his office.

## A SOLUTION

The head pretended he was angry. Paul's first action was to ask him not to shout. He stopped and calmed down. Paul's second action was to explain he had not noticed the school was at prayer and to apologise for his mistake. The affair ended there.

What happened was that the fourteen-year-old *re-framed* the head. He rightly felt that the man was not really angry and he called his bluff. He then stepped out of the 'frightened child' role and apologised in an adult way. He effectively transformed the nature of the encounter.

See *Change* (Watzlawick 1974) for a beautiful historical example of re-framing.

An officer in the French Revolution was ordered to fire on the rabble in a square. He climbed on a wall and shouted: 'I have orders to fire on the rabble in this square – can all decent citizens leave the square as fast as they can so we have a clear view of the rabble!' The place was empty in three minutes.

Re-framing, or imposing a new mapping on a situation, is one of the most self-confident human strategies we know of.

## 6.3 THEY *CAN* DO IT

### SITUATION

Sue Leather[†] writes:

My idea was for the Cambridge First Certificate class to give two-minute talks in preparation for the oral part of the exam. I was aware that some of the Japanese women were really trying to avoid this ordeal by the use of varied and ingenious tactics. As the day approached when I would inevitably ask them to prepare a talk for the next day, their quiet reluctance turned to despair. Two of them even ambushed me in the lunch queue to try to persuade me that this was really not a good idea.

### A SOLUTION

I did not relent. I knew that I was putting them in what, for them, is a squirm-inducing situation by making them, however briefly, the centre of attention. I knew that I was embarrassing them and furthermore being completely heartless by not listening to their pleas. Actually, that's not true. I did listen. I just hung on and hoped, trusted that they would come up with the goods. It meant also being confident that they wouldn't dislike me for torturing them in this way. In refusing their requests I tried to convey some of my confidence to them. I found eye-contact and smiles to be more reassuring than words.

The three Japanese women gave truly spellbinding talks*, all on subjects which were obviously very real to them. For the first time in the stories, the listeners listened because they really became involved in the stories, rather than because I had told them to. The rewards of actually giving the talks was evident to the speakers on the faces of the listeners. It wasn't necessary for me to praise them, but I did anyway.

It is very easy to draw facile conclusions from all this, but much more difficult to say what is really going on. The only thing I can say is that I hope they have gained the confidence of knowing that what they have to say can be interesting to others. For my own part, I re-learnt the lesson that pushing a project through, and not being put off by threats of unpopularity, is an important part of being a teacher. It gave me confidence too.

* One of the girls demonstrated the use of an abacus and explained the system. The second told us about arranged marriages in Japan. The third told us about her feelings towards bikes and how her bike had been stolen the day she left Cambridge for continental Europe.

### NOTES

†Sue Leather, Director of Studies at Cambridge Academy of English. (See Bibliography for details of published work.)

## 6.4 LIGHT CONTRADICTIONS

### SITUATION

The class were mostly post-beginner teenagers. 'Rosie' was in her late fifties – back in her own country she looked after an ageing mother. Linguistically she was one of the weaker students in the group.

She sought to gain the teacher's attention at all times. At breaks she would continually ask questions and request advice. At the start of each activity she would ritually say, without regard to the task in hand: *It's difficult*. Paul found this disconcerting and these labellings had a negative influence on the rest of the class. Rosie's negative self-image meant that she seldom did an activity well and to a certain extent disrupted her neighbours.

### A SOLUTION

Paul writes:

After a few days I decided to contradict her. As I gave out photocopies of a lesson, sure enough, as soon as she grasped her copy, she said without thinking or even looking at the sheet: 'Oh, this is difficult'. I stared at her and then said: 'No, it's impossible for you'. She stared back a little startled, my tone of voice had suggested I wasn't serious (if I had been I wouldn't have said it). 'But it *is* difficult', she replied. I answered: 'Yes, that's what I said. It's impossible for you', still in a light tone. The class was generally interested in what would happen next. I surmised that some were a little aghast that a teacher should mistreat an elderly student so. Some students who had been on the point of getting annoyed by her fussiness were now rallying in solidarity with her. 'No, it is difficult but it's not impossible. I can do it', she replied. She and the students then settled down to the activity. Rosie performed very well and the class generally did the activity much better than I had anticipated.

Over the next couple of weeks Rosie frequently repeated her distress signal: 'It's difficult'. I gently and lightly but firmly contradicted her: 'It's impossible for you because you're too old'. She not so gently but still firmly contradicted me. 'No, it's not impossible, I can!' Her attitude changed, she now got on better with the other students (who had begun to be a little patronising), performed well in class and after some initial difficulties also got the hang of self-study. The students in the class supported her when she had genuine difficulty and she supported them when they had boy/girlfriend trouble. She stopped saying, 'It's difficult'. On the last day she said, 'It was difficult but I could do it'.

## 6.5 THE SILENT WOMAN

### SITUATION

As Kevin perceived it his class was a boring, traditionalist one. They would not let him, as the teacher, do anything interesting in the morning. They insisted on grammar first thing. The mood of the class that day was apathetic and sleepy. As he went in, Kevin was particularly aware of being peeved with A, a Japanese woman who never spoke.

### A SOLUTION

Kevin started the lesson with a grammar exercise. He asked A the first question. She complied with reasonably awful intonation and pronunciation. He asked her the second question. She asked, *Why me?* this time with near perfect intonation. She complied. The class perked up a bit. Kevin calmly asked her a third question – the class were really listening – A protested loudly, *It's not fair*, etc. Once again her intonation and pronunciation were excellent. Kevin asked her a further string of questions. Now the class was awake and the Japanese woman had broken her silence. A negative pattern had been fractured.

### NOTES

Kevin decided to use a relatively aggressive insistence or forcing technique while he was himself in the grip of negative, aggressive feelings. That day it worked out OK for him. If you decide to use forcing techniques it is sensible for you to be in a calm, neutral mood, not an angry one.

## 6.6 COPING WITH A COLLEAGUE

### SITUATION

Sometimes I find it hard to cope with a colleague's reaction to a particular student in a class we share. E is from a broken home. Two years ago she nearly killed herself by compulsive fasting. She has a strong personality and can disturb many of her classmates both by drifting off and by disruptive tactics. She needs to be the centre of the party. My colleague, W, disliked her from the very first lesson. W's dislike for her annoys me and makes me listen to W less attentively on other matters.

### A SOLUTION

One morning E arrived five minutes late. I decided to try and see her through W's eyes. I made a mental effort to feel myself in W's style of clothes, to stand as she stands, to assume her movements. I decided to see E through W's negative spectacles.

The sensation of viewing E this way was very powerful. I revelled in an unfettered feeling of straight dislike. What probably happened was that the role-reversal into my fantasy of what W perceives and feels allowed me to guiltlessly live aggressive feelings towards E that I normally squash and push away in order to be able to work with her. The joy of this experience is that I feel a lot better now with W. The animosity has peeled away.

I am an angry person and find role-reversal into the other person's shoes a good way of dealing with my threatening, negative feelings. I often do this when someone riles me in class. Once I have partly perceived the situation from their side the anger attenuates. To put myself in their shoes, I try to assume the same breathing rate* as them and to mentally feel my body in the same posture as theirs (it is often not possible to physically take up the same position as I would be seen to be aping them).

* Herbert Puchta warns that assuming the same breathing rate as another may get you too close to them for you own good. He paces the other's breathing with a finger. (See Bibliography for details of published work).

## 6.7 ACTING OUT

### SITUATION

N's father was head of a family firm. She was twenty and worked for him. When you met her, her bearing and her clothes seemed too young for her age.

These were her father's instructions to the principal of the school in the UK he brought her to:

- N wants to learn English
- She is twenty but acts like a child
- She will stay in the UK for four months
- If she misses a class or does not work, I am to be phoned at once
- She needs watching

N's way of coping with this situation was to withdraw and refuse to let on she knew any English (she was upper intermediate.) Over the first month her blank negativism disturbed the class.

### A SOLUTION

At the end of one particularly bad lesson the teacher took N and one of her classmates, G, aside. He suggested that it was about time she began thinking of kneeing her father where it hurts. He suggested that she pretend to try it out on G. When she realised what he was suggesting she started laughing and laughing and saying she couldn't possibly. The teacher then role play demonstrated on G, who was happy to try and move the N situation. In the end, as a kind of joke, she did try.

This bit of after-class displaced acting out did not make N a happy student for the following three months. It did, though, somehow alleviate the situation for her, for the others and for the teacher. It was a way of stating and admitting part of the root problem.

## 6.8 AN ABSENT VOICE

### SITUATION

This was a business English option and A was asked to give a report on a chapter from a book on pricing. She had read the chapter and mastered the ideas, some of which were new to her and to the group. When she started speaking it was not really *to* the group, more *at* them. Her voice was high-pitched and artificial and there was no eye-contact. It was the kind of self-presentation induced by those dreadful Italian oral examinations of students in front of a somnolent class. Within a couple of minutes she had lost the group's attention, as her voice said, *Don't listen,* as strongly as her ideas were saying, *Please listen.*

### A SOLUTION

The teacher stopped A and explained that she was really not coming across. He asked her to choose a person in the group she could talk to easily. She did, with a glance rather than words. The teacher asked her to address G, to imagine he was ten and so explain things simply, and to forget the rest of the group. G helped by sucking his thumb!

The change was dramatic. Her voice came back into its normal warm, friendly self. The group were now able to follow the complex ideas about pricing. She was clearly very relieved and had learnt a technique she can use next time she is faced with addressing a group.

## 6.9 A CASE OF CONSONANT CLUSTERS

### SITUATION

U was a cheerful, outgoing person from Thailand. She was in her early twenties and had a good degree in politics – her reading knowledge of English was excellent. The problem was that, though she had started English in nursery school, no one in the UK could understand her. Her landlady's family complained she was unintelligible and classmates' eyes would glaze over when she began to speak. For her it was like experiencing dumbness, and after ten days of this she was depressed and shaken.

### A SOLUTION

We began to work together in the lunch break to achieve three technical aims:
- for U to pronounce the second half of words
- for her to produce consonant clusters
- for her to improve her stress and intonation

We tried many ways of doing this:

a  The 'elder sister' system; I got another Thai girl, with good pronunciation, to help her with hard sounds. I identified a problem area, checked that D was an adequate model and then left them alone for three or four minutes to work on the difficulty.

**b** I gave U dictations in which she only took down the last three letters of each word: __ese, _____ons, ___ked, _ike, _his!

**c** We did a range of drama exercises.

After ten days of this work U reported that her landlady could understand her better now. Her face was happier – some confidence had been restored.

Though her problem was technical the solution was only partly so. A major factor was that D and I gave up twenty minutes of the lunch-break to help her. The proof of the importance of the affective side of things was that when I stopped the lunchtime sessions half-way through term, U became less strongly present in the class group and began missing classes now and then. The problem was technical but the solution was more than technical.

# 6.10 A HELPLESS HELPER

## SITUATION

K was late for the test at the beginning of term. He seemed to find the questions very hard to read. He kept calling me over to read questions to him. Once he heard them he had no difficulty answering.

K speaks fluent, idiomatic English. He has learnt most of it from native and not from EFL-ridden classrooms. He is by far the best speaker in his Cambridge First Certificate exam class. He can confidently read and spell words of up to three and four letters, but words like *bridge* and *first* are beyond him.

The problem was that I felt a driving urge to help him. To do this I had to:

- establish a strong rapport with him
- persuade him to read extensively
- focus him on spelling

To get rapport I asked him to teach me Arabic writing in return for English spelling lessons, and to get him to read I gave him an erotic novel. We had three sessions together and then he stopped coming, without a word. I felt angry.

## A SOLUTION

I have to cope with my need to 'help', as clearly this drive is a lot stronger than K's to learn to read and write English. I need to equanimously accept the failure of this intervention and be grateful to K for making me aware of an unuseful need in myself. His silent disappearance after the third meeting had a strange, arrogant dignity.

## 6.11 LOSS OF STATUS

### SITUATION

When a doctor cures a patient, the latter is grateful but usually none the wiser technically. When a lawyer wins a case for his client, the former is confirmed in his status as a successful expert.

When language teachers take a beginner to proficiency level, they make the learner so like themself that they lose their status as arcane experts, the holders of hidden knowledge and skill. This is the way a colleague of ours, Jim Brims, put it, speaking of an Arab student of his:

When I first met him he could hardly put two words together in English. I haven't seen him over the last few months and then yesterday I bumped into him; he was using really colloquial phrases and understanding everything I said to him – I was no longer towering above him like I did when he was a beginner.

### A SOLUTION

Charles Curran, the inventor of Community Language Learning, understands the feeling of loss experienced by the teacher quoted above. Curran sees teachers of beginners as giants among pygmies, which means they should adopt a very low-profile, non-dominant stance. As students gradually learn more and more, the onus is on them to reassure the fallen giants, their teachers, by offering them the respect due to an expert and by valuing their detailed knowledge of the subject.

### NOTES

Neither of the authors have direct experience of the problem outlined here. However, this book is about the insecurity and confidence of a wide range of people, not just feelings we ourselves can directly access.

ACKNOWLEDGEMENT
Jim Brims does not think he *should* feel the way he feels – he just does (See Bibliography for details of published work).

## 6.12 DEFENSIVE TEACHING

### SITUATION

If you are a trainee teacher being inspected by your tutor, you may well teach defensively. You will do all the things to please them that you can. You are teaching for the tutor, not for the students and not for yourself. If you are a state school teacher and the inspector is due, you may well have tapped the grapevine to find out what style of lesson they seem to go for. Again, the lesson addressee will be an extraneous third party.

Teacher B started work in a school on a temporary contract. It was a small private language school and the principal was very eager to please his customers. A student from B's class went to the principal and asked to move up a class. B said he did not think that the student was substantially better than the rest of the class but the principal moved the student anyway. The first student's friend also went and got a move from the principal and so did a third student. Things were beginning to look bad. B changed his lessons slightly, making them a little hard for the class and packed with more material than the students could cope with. No more students left the class and B was re-employed for a further term. He has a secure job now, but his lessons, although well planned, are just a little bit above the level of the class and he covers much more material than you would expect.

## A SOLUTION

Sometimes go into class without the armour of a planned lesson. Know the area you want to work in, explain this to the students, but let the work you do arise out of the situation in the group. Take a risk and let the lesson be for you, for them and not for the ghost of your initial trainer. The best lessons are for the students and the teacher, not for third party super-egos.

# 6.13 POSTSCRIPT

When dealing with a 'problem' student these guidelines may be of help:
- Take time to listen to and talk to the student.
- Give the person the chance to really say how they feel and clear the ground for their own thinking. Just listen – do not intervene, justify, divert.
- Help the student to brainstorm all possible solutions, however apparently wild.
- Suggest that the student chooses a course of action and puts it into practice. There should be something contractual about this choice.

A good source for further reading in this area is *Working with Uncertainty* (Dixon and Gordon 1987).

# Bibliography

Agosta, J 1988 *Changing Energies* Pilgrims Publications

Bald, W-D, Cobb, D and Schwarz, A 1986 *Active Grammar* Longman

Bandler, R and Grinder, J 1975 *The Structure of Magic* **1** and **2** Science and behaviour

Bowers, RG, Bamber, B, Straker Cook, R and Thomas, AL 1987 *Talking about Grammar* Longman

Brims, J 1988 *Speaking 4* Cassell

Creton, J-P 1983 *Day by Day* Pilgrims Publications

Davis P and Rinvolucri, M 1988 *Dictation* CUP

Dixon, H and Gordon, P 1987 *Working with Uncertainty* FPA Education Unit/Cambridge Health Authority

Eastwood, J and Mackin, R 1982 *A Basic English Grammar* OUP

Gattegno, C 1972 *Teaching Foreign Languages in Schools – the Silent Way* Educational Solutions

Hedge, T 1988 *Writing* OUP

Heron, J 1975 *Six Category Intervention Analysis* Surrey University

Houston, G 1984 *The Red Book of Groups* (obtainable from the author, 8 Rochester Terrace, London NW1 9JN)

Kohl, H 1977 *Writing, Maths and Games in the Open Classroom* Methuen

Lavery, M 1984 *Active Viewing Plus* Modern English Publications/ Macmillan

Lavery, M (forthcoming) *Video* OUP

Leather, S 1989 *Desert, Mountain, Sea* OUP

Longfellow, H 1982 The Rainy Day. In *The Poetical Works of Henry H Longfellow* Suttaby and Co.

Morgan, J and Rinvolucri, M 1984 *Once Upon a Time* CUP

Morgan, J and Rinvolucri, M 1988 *The Q Book* Longman

Morgan, J and Rinvolucri, M 1986 *Vocabulary* OUP

Moskowitz, G 1978 *Caring and Sharing in the Foreign Language Classroom* Newbury House

Pitcher, EG and Prelinger, E 1969 *Children Tell Stories* International Universities Press

Puchta, H and Schratz, M (forthcoming) *Active Learning* Longman

Rees Miller, J (ed.) (forthcoming) *Development for Teachers not Trainers* OUP

Rinvolucri, M 1988 A Role Switching Exercise in Teacher Training *Modern English Teacher*

Rogers, C 1983 *Freedom to Learn for the Eighties* Charles E Merrill

Spaventa, L (ed.) 1980 *Towards the Creative Teaching of English* Heinemann

Swan M 1980 *Practical English Usage* OUP

Syer, J and Connolly, C 1984 *Sporting body, Sporting Mind* CUP

Szkutnik, LL 1986 *Thinking in English* Panstwowe Wydawhictwo Nauhowe

Watzlawick, P 1974 *Change* WW Norton

Woodward, T 1990 *Models and Metaphors* in *Language Teacher Training* CUP, revised and expanded from *Loop Input* 1988 Pilgrims Publications

# Further reading

Cassidy, J and Rimbeaux, BC 1983 *Juggling for the Complete Klutz* Fontana

Cleveland, BF 1984 *Master Teaching Techniques* Connecting Link Press

Dickson, A 1983 *A Woman in Your Own Right* Quartet Books

Fanselow, J 1987 *Breaking Rules* Longman

Harrison, BT 1986 *Sarah's Letters: A Case of Shyness* Bedford Way Papers

Quinn, K 1983 *Stand Your Ground* Orbis Publishing

Stanworth, M 1983 *Gender and Schooling* Hutchinson